DESIGNED
FOR
DESTINY

Linda Santangelo

Acknowledgments

After publishing the first book, *Secrets Revealed*, in December 2017, I received a prophetic word that more books would be written and they would come quickly. This year, I received two words within four days that it was time to write the second book.

Thank You, Lord, for speaking to me about writing this book, for giving me the topic, and for the Holy Spirit downloads that breathed the words onto these pages. My first book was a struggle to complete, but this one flowed quickly. My prayer is that You will use it to transform lives!

I wish to thank, Marios Ellinas, Angela Muncie, and Barbara Monroe for speaking prophetically, in birthing this book, by confirming the timing of the Lord and content.

My husband is so tolerant of all the time it takes to write a book. Thank you, Vinnie, for your support and understanding! I love you...

Thank you Marios Ellinas for all the words and sage advice you've given this new author. I so appreciate your friendship!

I am also grateful to Dineen Miller for a cover design that creatively expresses the divine destiny God has for each one of us that comes from heaven to earth.

Michele Gunn, I'm thankful for that blessed Kairos moment

the Lord brought us together in answer to my prayer to find an editor. My heart is filled with gratefulness for your help to portray what was in my spirit with clear and concise wording. Your advice has been invaluable.

I am also thankful for Kathy Brooks' help and friendship.

Foreword

God has a destiny for you, but it comes with a price; the price for the place is preparation! This book, *Designed for Destiny*, is *great* preparation for that destiny! I have known Linda, partnered with her in ministry, and have personally been enriched by her inner healing ministry within Reformation Center. Linda carries and lives what she's authored here. I personally know numerous people who have had their lives transformed by the power of the Holy Spirit through her ministry, and I know your destiny will be greatly liberated on the other side of this book.

I love that *Designed for Destiny* is not just information, but also activation! Most people I talk with have a sense that they should be beyond where they currently are in their life – feeling that God has more for them. But most aren't aware of what's keeping them from it! Many others are aware, but not sure how to navigate beyond it. If that's you and you're looking to fully release your God given destiny, then I say "read on!" Each chapter is pregnant with breakthrough!

I'd like to challenge you to not just read this book but listen to the Holy Spirit minister to you as you read. Then, make time to really process the activations at the end of each chapter. It's not just your destiny that's at stake but also the destinies of all of those lives *you* will touch as a result of walking deeper into your destiny.

Ron Kutinsky – Sr. Leader of Hope International Ministries
Author of: *Breaking the Barrier of Average*

ALL THE DAYS ORDAINED FOR ME
WERE WRITTEN IN YOUR BOOK BEFORE
ONE OF THEM CAME TO BE.
PSALM 139:16 (NIV)

Table of Contents

Introduction

We have a destiny to fulfill during our time on earth because we have all been *Designed for Destiny*. So many of us fall short of achieving all that has been placed within our hearts to accomplish and have no idea what God has predestined us to do. I was one of those who didn't believe I could accomplish much for the Kingdom of God. You see, I was stuck in a system of wrong beliefs, attitudes, and many hindrances in my life that held me back from seeing I even had a destiny.

Even if I understood I had a destiny, I didn't understand how to get beyond what was standing in the way of that destiny being fully realized. The Word of God addresses the importance of character, but many Christians who know these Bible verses are unable to walk in God's principles.

This is a new season where the Spirit is illuminating the way to transformation. He is showing us that we don't have to live with the things holding us back from the great destiny God has in store for us.

There is a quickening of great desire arising in the body of Christ to know and understand why we are living so far below the call of God. We are beginning to suspect that God has more in store for us than what we have seen. Hope is springing forth and we are looking for answers to the cry of our hearts.

This book will help us understand many things that are holding us back from seeing or believing the destiny God has in His heart for us. We will learn how to remove these hindrances and obstacles so we can fulfill the call God has placed within us. He created us for a purpose and we are meant to walk in that purpose and find great contentment and delight in what He has in His heart for us to do.

We have been *"Designed for Destiny"*.

Chapter 1

DESTINY IS WRITTEN

"Your eyes saw my unformed body; all the days ordained for me were written in your book before one of them came to be."
Psalm 139:16 (NIV)

According to Psalm 139, before we ever came to be, all the plans, assignments, callings, gifting's, and anointing that comprise our destiny were written in a book in heaven with our name on it. We see, by this verse, we *are* truly *Designed for Destiny*! God so loves us that He has a wonderful, bright future planned for each of us which will yield such fulfillment, ignite much passion, create big dreams, and quicken the deep desires of our heart. The word used for 'book' in this verse translates 'scroll'.

This scroll of destiny is placed within our heart with a blueprint from heaven stamped upon the ancient pages of our predestined life.

It is ours for the taking, so why do we live so far below what is written in our book of destiny? We may live our lives never seeing our dreams and passions realized in our lifetime.

This book is written to answer this question and also to help release those who are hindered from walking in their destiny. We all have free will and can choose either to walk in the plan God has written in His book for us or to live our entire lifetime in mediocrity, never seeing our deepest heart's desires fulfilled. If we choose not to walk in God's plan, we will never rise to the heights of the great destiny He recorded in our scroll.

> *"Before I formed you in the womb I <u>knew</u> you, before you were born I <u>set you</u> <u>apart</u>; I <u>appointed</u> you as a prophet to the nations."*
> Jeremiah 1:5 (NIV)

Here we see that before the Lord formed Jeremiah in his mother's womb, He *knew* him, *called* him, and *appointed* him to be a prophet to the nations. What was written in Jeremiah's book, long before he was ever born, was that his destiny was to be a prophet. *What is written on the pages of your book about your life and destiny?*

We are about to take a trip to clear our road to destiny, of hindrances and obstacles which may prevent us from seeing and believing the beautiful plan God has written in our individual scrolls.

So many seem to be stuck and unable to move into mature growth in Christ.

> *"For those God foreknew He also predestined to be conformed to the image of His Son (Jesus)."*
> Romans 8:29

Not only do we have a book in heaven with our destiny written upon the pages, but we have been predestined to be conformed to the image of Jesus in all aspects. So why aren't we truly conformed to His image? Why don't we do the works of Jesus and even greater things, as we were promised in John 14:12?

There are so many reasons why this maturity in Christ can be hindered. We want to believe God and His transforming Word, but are unable to because we may have trust issues that prevent us from being able to trust God. Or perhaps we walk with anger issues which prevent us from being conformed to His image. There may be other things like fear that keep us from moving forward into this maturity. The Lord loves us and wants to set us free so we are able to hear, believe, and act upon the assignments and callings the Lord has written on our pages.

The avenue to releasing our destiny is through transformation.

Transformation is needed in every person's life in order to be conformed to the image of Christ. We received salvation when we believed in Christ, but it is a process to grow into the image of Christ. The good news is, it says in 2 Corinthians 2:18, we have been *created* to be transformed into His image from glory to glory.

There is healing and deliverance from *all* the things keeping us from being conformed to that image. God loves us way too much to leave us the way we are and wants to transform us from the things which prevent His purposes being lived out in our lives.

Without freedom and transformation, we will have a difficult time fulfilling our destiny because of the obstacles stemming from our unhealed pain and brokenness. These prevent us from being able to live out what is written in our book in heaven.

In this season, according to I Peter 1:16, we are being set aside and made holy, as God is holy. We must all come to the place where the character of Christ is being formed in us so we think like Him, speak like Him, and do what He did.

The Bible says of Jesus in I John 4:17 that, "*As He is, so also are we in this world.*" The truth is, we all need transformation in our lives to become as He is!

We need to come out of the strongholds that prevent us from being like Jesus in everything we do, as well as how we respond to and treat others. The Spirit is inviting us to come out of immature character. SOZO is the word used for salvation in the Bible and is defined as: *'safe, to save, i.e. deliver or protect (literally or figuratively): heal, preserve, save (self), do well, be (make) whole'* (Strong's #4982). So we *should* be healed, doing well and made whole, as this is part of our salvation.

We may find ourselves living to the best of our ability but still stuck in attitudes, thoughts, and responses that do not line up with the Word of God. We know the right things to do, but so many of us still do the opposite.

It's time to become world changers and live out the fantastic destiny written in our book.

It's also time to do the exploits of Jesus and even greater works than Jesus did to rock this world. It's time we become world changers and live out the fantastic destiny written in our book to accomplish the assignments God purposed for our life.

How do we get there from where we are? How do we change

the thoughts that keep us in prison so we can't do or believe what the Lord has destined us to do? What is being done to bring us into complete freedom from our wrong ways that are not conformed to the image of Christ?

This is where inner healing comes in to bring transformation. Physical healing is when Jesus heals a physical problem like our back pain or other ailments. The truth is, we all have emotional pain we suffer from in our lives that Jesus would also like to heal. This emotional healing has been termed *inner healing*. Inner healing is needed for us to be set free from those trust, anger, fear, insecurity, low self–esteem, and many other issues whose roots come from prior hurt and pain in our life.

Let's lay a scriptural foundation for inner healing and its importance.

"When He (Jesus) saw the crowds, He had compassion on them,
because they were harassed and helpless, like
sheep without a shepherd.
Matthew 9:36 (NIV)

To understand who Jesus was referring to in this verse, we need to understand what harassed means. It is defined: *'to be stressed out, worried, worn out, hard pressed, tormented with troubles or cares, bothered continually, persecuted, and troubled by repeated attacks.'* Certainly, these are people who sound like they *really* need inner healing in their lives. The Great news is that Jesus has compassion on us and wants to set us free from harassments! There is always hope and healing He wants to bring us. Isaiah 53:5 says, by Jesus' wounds we are healed.

There are so many children who have grown up in dysfunctional homes with the pain and brokenness it causes. The dysfunction continues into their adult lives because it's what they consider normal and may think, "That's just who I am." That is why we see so many people in Church who bite others or behave defensively, because *they* have been wounded. The great news is Jesus loves them and came to heal and deliver them.

"Wounded people wound people," but the good news is that after inner healing, "Healed people heal people."

"Some sat in utter darkness, prisoners suffering in iron chains and there was no one to help them. When they cried to the Lord in their trouble, He saved them from their distress. He brought them out of darkness and broke away their chains."
Psalm 107:10 &14 (NIV)

In John 10:10, it tells us that Satan comes to steal, kill, and destroy our lives, but Jesus came for us to have life and more abundantly. So when we cry out to the Lord in our trouble, He saves us from our distress, brings us out of darkness, and breaks away our chains. This is a perfect picture of His love for us in the ministry of Jesus through inner healing.

In the New Testament, Jesus says:

"The Spirit of the Lord is upon me, because He has anointed me to proclaim good news to the poor. He has sent me to proclaim liberty to the captives and recovery of sight to the blind, to set at liberty those who are oppressed, to proclaim the year of the Lord's favor."
Luke 4:18 (NIV)

Inner healing is good news to those who are held captive and oppressed, those who are downtrodden and harassed. Not only does the Lord want to heal diseases (recovery of sight to the blind), but he wants our emotions to be healed as well so that our *soul* prospers in all aspects. He has also anointed and appointed *us* to set the captives free and open their prison doors. In Luke 10:19, it says that He has given *us* all authority over the works of the enemy. We use that authority in inner healing *'to set at liberty those who are oppressed.'*

"Beloved, I pray that in all respects you may prosper and be in good health, just as your <u>soul</u> <u>prospers</u>."
3 John 1:2 (NASB)

"We pray that your whole self –spirit, <u>soul</u>, and body, will <u>be</u> <u>kept</u> <u>safe</u> <u>and</u> <u>be</u> <u>blameless</u> when our Lord Jesus Christ comes."
1 Thessalonians 5:23 (ESV)

Here in 3 John and 1Thessalonians, we see the importance of our soul being safe, blameless, and prospering. It is also understood from these verses that our soul may not be, if *they* needed to pray for our soul to be kept safe, blameless, and to prosper.

Jesus gave His life on the cross for the forgiveness of our sins.

"In Him (Jesus) we have redemption through His blood, the forgiveness of sins, in accordance with the riches of God's grace."
Ephesians 1:7 (NIV)

Our sins were forgiven by what Jesus did on the cross in giving His life for us, but the effects of that sin may still remain. For example, a mother may have thrown her son out of the house in anger, repented for it and received forgiveness, but the effect of her actions still remain until that relationship is restored. Her son, having issues of his own, may not be ready to have that relationship restored. Or a young man may have stolen something, repented for doing it and received forgiveness, but still have to serve jail time for stealing. There are so many other examples of how the effects of sin may remain even though we have been forgiven.

We may have had a difficult childhood, are now following Jesus, but still have the effects from those childhood experiences that hinder our peace, relationships, and the ability to fully move forward in our Christian walk. Jesus came to heal our soul, which is our mind, will and emotions, and when healed, our soul will prosper.

Science has determined that our identity is established during the first 12 years of life, where our *adult attitudes, thought processes, and responses* are forged in that season. Most painful memories are stored in our subconscious mind, which are pushed down and pretty much forgotten when we become adults. But the effects of these memories are still influencing our adult lives and become triggers that set off pain, which cause us to respond in hurtful or angry ways.

The reason we need inner healing is because of our unhealed wounds or pain, unmet needs of nurture or love, or any issues we have not resolved from our past.

In the midst of *all* these unhealed areas, God still has a wonderful destiny planned for us and wants to heal us and set us free from *every* obstacle that would prevent us from fully realizing and walking in that plan.

Lord, I declare those who are reading this book will begin to see and understand, because of Your exceeding goodness, the areas needing your healing and transformation. Open our eyes to see that which we have not seen and to understand what we have not understood about Your healing power, so our soul can begin to prosper.

In Jesus' name, Amen.

This lightning is symbolic of destiny that
comes from heaven to earth.

ALL THE DAYS ORDAINED FOR ME
WERE WRITTEN IN YOUR BOOK BEFORE
ONE OF THEM CAME TO BE.
PSALM 139:16 (NIV)

Chapter 2

OBSTACLES TO DESTINY

I would be remiss without exposing the *greatest* obstacle from walking in our destiny. Let's begin by talking about forgiveness, as it's extremely vital to our health and well–being. The lack of forgiveness becomes a huge obstacle to inner healing, as well as in being able to walk in our destiny. The Bible has a lot to say about this subject, and it's crucial to understand the *power of forgiveness* and the place it holds in our healing process. The core and foundation of inner healing is built upon the ability to forgive, so we *really* need to understand the significance it plays before we are able to go on to teach other parts of the healing process.

The disciples asked Jesus how to pray and in the Lord's Prayer, Jesus told them to pray in Luke 11:4, *"Forgive us our sins, as we forgive those who sin against us."* Jesus teaches us that forgiveness is of the utmost importance to our wholeness!

Unforgiveness is the greatest obstacle to walking in freedom and wholeness.

Unforgiveness is one of the greatest hindrances to inner healing and has to be dealt with in order to be at peace and walk in freedom. It also causes all kinds of illness and disease which creates pain and misery in those who don't forgive.

Some of the illnesses scientists have found frequently associated with roots of unforgiveness/bitterness are:

- high blood pressure
- heart disease
- cancer
- bone disease
- arthritis
- autoimmune disease
- other illnesses

All illnesses are not healed during inner healing, but sometimes those rooted in stress, emotional pain, unforgiveness, or bitterness may be healed during inner healing prayer.

I remember a man who came forward on a Sunday morning and wanted prayer for back pain. After praying for him several times, the pain was still as intense as when we started. I asked the Lord if something needed to be seen and I heard the word, *bitterness,* and asked the man if anyone had hurt him recently. He told us about a bad break in a relationship and how much he had been hurt. I asked if he had forgiven the person for what they had done and shared that possibly the pain was related to this. He was willing to forgive and after leading him in prayer, I told him we would pray for his back again. The man replied that it wasn't necessary as his pain was now healed. The bitterness left when he forgave the person who hurt him and he was instantaneously healed without any additional prayer for the pain.

We can see how sometimes unforgiveness and bitterness is tied to our illnesses and pain. It says in Hebrews 12:15 (NLT),

> *"Look after each other so that none of you fails to receive the grace of God. <u>Watch</u> <u>out</u> <u>that</u> <u>no</u> <u>poisonous</u> <u>root</u> <u>of</u> <u>bitterness</u> <u>grows</u> <u>up</u> <u>to</u> <u>trouble</u> <u>you</u>, corrupting many."*

When we walk in unforgiveness, we walk in *great* deception. It's like drinking deadly poison and expecting the *other* person to die! Really, the only one unforgiveness hurts is the one who won't forgive. The other person is going on with their life never thinking about us, but we have offenses that we are holding against them which cause *us* to be miserable.

The truth is that forgiveness is what brings us back into relationship with God and others. It's always a choice as God never forces us to forgive, but the choice to not forgive always comes with a great cost.

> *"For if you forgive men when they sin against you, your heavenly Father will also forgive you. But if you do not forgive men their sins, your Father will not forgive your sins."*
> Matthew 6:14-15 (NIV)

Wow! I sure know I want my sins forgiven and the way for that to happen is to forgive others when they sin against me. Unforgiveness always starts when we become offended by another person's words or actions, hold on to that offense, and enter into unforgiveness for what they did to us. Resentment and bitterness set in and then we are tormented and miserable.

Lamentations 3:22–23 tells us that God's love for us is totally unconditional. His forgiveness is not, according to Jesus in Matthew 6. We are called to live both forgiven by God and forgiving of others.

> *"Then Peter came to Jesus and asked, 'Lord, how many times*
> *shall I forgive my brother or sister who sins against me?*
> *Up to seven times?' Jesus answered, 'I tell you, not seven*
> *times, but seventy times seven.'"*
> Matthew 18:21-22 (NIV)

That's 490 times and a *whole* lot of forgiveness! Jesus goes on to teach them about a servant who owed a lot of money to his master. When the servant asked for forgiveness of the large debt, he was forgiven and went out a very happy man. This same servant had someone who owed him a small amount of money and when that person asked to be forgiven *his* debt, the servant refused him and had him thrown in prison. The master heard what happened and became very angry.

God is the Master in this parable Who, because of His great love for us, forgave *all* our sins. When we have been forgiven for every single thing we have ever done wrong, we should not withhold forgiveness from others who have wronged us.

> *"Then the master (God) called the servant in. 'You wicked*
> *servant,' he said, 'I canceled all that debt of yours*
> *because you begged me to. <u>Shouldn't you have had</u>*
> *<u>mercy on your fellow servant just as I had on you?'</u>*
> *In anger his <u>master handed him over to the jailers to</u>*
> *<u>be tortured</u>, until he should pay back all he owed.*
> Matthew 18:32–34 (NIV)

In verse 35 of the same chapter, Jesus says,

> *"This is how my heavenly Father will treat each of you unless*
> *you forgive your brother or sister from your heart."*

This is powerful stuff! Jesus uses this parable to demonstrate to us what happens when we don't forgive others for what they have said or done to us. In verse 34 the jailer is *Satan*, who tortures us by making us *miserable* and as we saw, we may become physically ill because of our unwillingness to forgive others. Remember, Satan comes to steal, kill, and destroy our lives and unforgiveness is one of his tools to accomplish that. He wants to keep us in unforgiveness so we are *miserable* and *ineffective* for the Kingdom of God. It doesn't have to be this way!

Unforgiveness puts a wall between us and God.

Unforgiveness also puts a wall between us and God; the Word says, because we don't forgive others, our sins can't be forgiven. We wonder why we don't feel as close to God as we would like, but don't understand why. There truly are Kingdom principles that operate in our lives even when we don't understand them.

So what is buried behind that wall of unforgiveness toward others? What is hiding in our life that we are not seeing? There is a progression of results that originate from an offense, which we call the unforgiveness cycle:

- offenses
- unforgiveness
- bitterness
- possibly jealousy
- resentment
- retaliation/revenge/judgment
- anger/wrath/rage
- hatred
- violence
- murder/accusation

It always starts with an *offense* we receive and then we enter into unforgiveness toward the person. The unforgiveness progresses into bitterness, or even jealousy, and then resentment happens. If the process isn't stopped by forgiving them, we begin to retaliate in either thought or actions that lead to revenge and judgment. We then move into anger, wrath, rage, and progress to hatred, violence, accusations, and even murder with thought or deed. That violence or murder can also be accomplished by our words in character assassination through gossip. We begin to tell others how that person has wronged us and how terrible they are for treating us this way. This is the progression of what unforgiveness does in our lives. It is *extremely* harmful to our peace, mental and emotional well-being, as well as our physical health.

Many times we don't even recognize who we need to forgive because it is *buried* in our subconscious and not visible. So here are some signs that we may carry unforgiveness toward others.

- There are people we can't talk about without becoming upset.
- When we think about them or see them, we have a tightness in our stomach.
- We avoid them when we see them coming or pretend we don't see them.
- We speak with an angry tone in our voice, or with constant negativity about them.
- We have judgmental and critical thoughts or gossip to others about them.

Some of our more difficult forgiveness issues come from forgiving our parents, other immediate family members, or even someone who has abused us earlier in our childhood. *Inner healing helps us through the forgiveness process* so we able to forgive those who *deeply* hurt us and caused such pain in our life.

So who is it we need to forgive? Do we need to forgive another person? Perhaps we need to forgive God, or even ourselves.

We may not even be aware that we are angry at God for a situation, disappointment, unmet expectation, and more. This can become a huge wall between us and our Heavenly Father. Then we wonder why we can't feel close to Him or have the relationship we desire with Him. This becomes a stumbling block and hindrance in our walk with God and our relationship.

I know a couple who were on the mission field serving God when their baby died. The relationship the man had with God changed after that. They left the mission field and sometime later, his wife thought he should seek inner healing. He came in but believed there wasn't anything that needed healing in his life. The Lord revealed deep down, he was angry toward God and felt because he was serving Him on the mission field, he couldn't understand why his baby died. He was *surprised* and didn't even realize this was buried deep within his subconscious. It was hidden because he felt it was wrong to be angry at God. When we led him in a prayer of forgiving God because he blamed Him for the death of his baby, he was totally healed and the wall between him and God came down. He is now experiencing such freedom in his life and has a close relationship with God once again.

Perhaps our need is to forgive ourselves; maybe we have failed in an area of our life, or we don't like ourselves, and possibly even hate ourselves. We may not like what we did, should have done, or didn't do. This can go all the way back to the womb as a powerful root for rejection and lack of self-worth that we hold against ourselves.

I lived in self–hatred much of my life. I hated my personality, my appearance, and the things I did or didn't do. I was harder on myself than God ever was and during my earlier years, many people told me this. I required a *lot* of inner healing to break down this self–destructive cycle in order to be who I am today. I needed to forgive *myself* for so many things and to receive the love of God to replace all my perceived failings. He also gave me a new identity! The good news is, by the grace of God, I am no longer the person I was back then. There *is* help and hope by walking in a lifestyle of forgiveness.

The Lord's commandment in Mark 12:31 is that we are to love one another *as* we love ourselves. If we don't love ourselves, then we can't love others the way God says we should. The word also says in 1 John 4:20, whoever does not love their brother and sister whom they have seen, cannot love God Whom they have not seen. Do we see how this all works together? We need to love others as we love ourselves and if we don't love others, we can't love God.

Most unforgiveness is hidden within our hearts, pushed down to where we don't even realize it's there, hindering everything we do.

It takes the work of the Holy Spirit to bring to light those we need to forgive.

Sometimes we may believe if we forgive someone, it means that what they did was okay; this is far from the truth and what they did was not okay! Forgiveness is really for our own sake because it frees us from the *misery* we feel and puts *us* in a place of *peace*. It reconciles us back to the Lord and also removes the hook that Satan put in us to keep us from walking in freedom.

> *"If you forgive anyone's sins, their sins are forgiven; if you*
> *do not forgive them, they are not forgiven."*
> John 20:23 (NIV)

We have the power to forgive the sins of others so those sins no longer torment us and cause us to be miserable. This verse also says if we don't forgive them, then those sins are not forgiven. We will continue in our misery and torment if we don't forgive them their sins, but it's totally up to us. For *we* hold this power to either forgive or not forgive those who sin against us. Remember Jesus said, "*Father forgive us our sins as we forgive those who sin against us.*" The price is too great a cost for us to hold on to unforgiveness.

Jesus also said in Luke 23:24, "*Father forgive them, for they know not what they do.*" If Jesus forgave those who were nailing Him to a cross, how much more should we forgive others and realize they *also* don't know what they are doing to *us*. They just may be so wounded and will continue to wound others because of *their* own pain.

We may be someone who feels we just can't forgive someone for what they did to us. When beginning to understand the inner healing ministry, the Lord spoke to me and said,

> **"You know how you are always hearing people say, 'I can**
> **never forgive them for what they did?' When they**
> **are healed and no longer have pain from what**
> **was done, it will be *easy* for them to forgive."**

It is actually the pain of what was done that keeps us from

being able to forgive the wrongdoer. But with the Lord's healing, we can forgive even the most painful situations. When Jesus removes the pain, it becomes easy to forgive the person who caused that pain.

Remember, unforgiveness is the greatest obstacle to inner healing and stands in the way of our destiny.

Jesus said in John 14:30 about Himself, the enemy has no place in Him or nothing in Him. I asked the Lord to show me what this meant and He revealed that Satan had no place in Jesus because he was sinless, but *also* because He had no unresolved *issues* in his life. So there was no place for Satan to operate, torment, or control Him. In all of the unhealed areas of *our* life, we give Satan a place in *us* to operate, torment, or control us. Unforgiveness is one of those places!

PRAYER OF FORGIVENESS:

Take a moment to ask the Holy Spirit to show you who you need to forgive, write their names down, and pray this prayer of forgiveness. *Do this for others, for God, and for yourself....*

FOR OTHERS:

Lord Jesus, I repent for the unforgiveness I have held in my heart toward _____. I also repent for the offenses, bitterness, jealousy, resentment, retaliation, revenge, judgment, anger, wrath, rage, hatred, violence, accusations, and murder I have thought or spoken about them. Repenting means *'turning away from'*, and I ask for Your help to stop the unforgiveness cycle.

Lord, I choose to forgive them for what they did or said to me and no longer hold them accountable for their sins. I choose to say like Jesus, *'Father forgive them for they did not know what they were doing.'*

I break all the sowing and reaping that has been in my life due to my unforgiveness. Not only do I forgive them, but I pray blessings over their life to obey the Word in Luke 6:28 that says to bless those who curse you and pray for those who mistreat you.

Thank You, Jesus, for forgiving my sin; help me to keep short accounts toward others who offend me. Heal all those stony places in my heart that cause me to stumble.

I thank You, in the name of Jesus, Amen....

FOR GOD:

I repent for the unforgiveness I have held in my heart toward You, Lord, for _____. I have held a wrong view of Who You are, and what Your motives are. I want to reconcile my relationship with You once again.

I forgive You, for You are a good Father and everything You do is good even if I don't understand it. Your Word in Romans 8:28 tells me that You work all things together for my good because I am called according to Your purpose.

I no longer hold You accountable, choose to trust You, and believe You have my best interest at heart.

I break all the sowing and reaping that has been in my life due to my wrong perspective of Who You are. You are a loving

God Who gave me everything so I may have life and have it more abundantly!

I submit myself to You and receive Your love!

I thank You, in the name of Jesus, Amen....

FOR MYSELF:

I repent for the unforgiveness I have held in my heart toward myself. I also repent for the offenses, bitterness, resentment, retaliation, revenge, judgment, anger, wrath, rage, hatred, violence, murder, and accusations I have thought or spoken about myself.

Lord, I choose to forgive myself for what I did or didn't do. _____ (name any actions or words you can recall), and no longer hold myself accountable for my sins. You came to take my punishment through Your death so I no longer have to pay the price. I choose to say like Jesus, "Father forgive me for I didn't know what I was doing."

I break all the sowing and reaping that has been in my life due to my unforgiveness. Not only do I forgive myself, but I pray blessings over my life from this day forth.

I thank You, in the name of Jesus, Amen...

Chapter 3

FRUITS AND ROOTS

Now that we have laid the foundation of forgiveness and its importance, let's continue in understanding the fruits and roots in our lives.

We hear people say, "That's just the way I am." This sentence usually means the person expects others to leave them alone so they don't have to deal with their issues and their past, or they feel so defeated and criticized, they don't think they can change. We may feel helpless, hopeless, and believe this is the way we are and can't change, but there is *great* help, hope, and healing in this book for us.

We have heard the old adage, *'Time heals all wounds.'* Actually, time doesn't heal all wounds. It only causes us to forget why we do the things we do, and how we've become who we are. The wounds are all still there, buried and festering in our subconscious. When someone says or does something that reminds our soul of that wounding, it triggers the pain of our past hurt to affect our present circumstance. When that button is pushed, the pain of that unhealed area affects how we now respond to our present circumstance. Actually, the wrong response we see today is the fruit, but the root we can't see is that unhealed wound from our childhood.

A good example of this is that our father may have left us as a young child. As adults, when we feel someone is abandoning us, it triggers that pain and fear from the past. This leads to angry thoughts, feelings, or outbursts in our present circumstances; so we transfer our responses to people who don't deserve them. We may never understand why we feel the way we do, but still have these negative feelings and responses to others. We may think, "That's just the way I am!" These feelings also become a block between us and God because we also transfer our feelings of abandonment to Him, and believe He is never there when we need Him. We can't figure out why we can't trust Him when the Word of God and our own intellect say we can! We enter into great internal conflict and become double–minded. The Bible says in James 1:8 that a double-minded man won't receive anything from God and is unstable in all his ways. So we wonder, "What is going on with me?"

I know someone whose father died when he was 10 years old, where he felt tremendous loss and abandonment. As an adult, every time his wife would want to visit family or go out with friends, it would trigger those old unhealed feelings in him. That familiar fear of being abandoned would return and he would become angry and resentful toward his wife. He had no clue why he felt like that, as he was just responding to present circumstances without understanding why he responded the way he did. He was perceived as being controlling but actually needed inner healing. Inner healing removes these effects from our lives, responses are transformed, and relationships healed.

Someone who felt rejected as a child now hears everything through a filter of rejection.

When someone says or does something to us that triggers old childhood feelings of rejection, we become easily hurt, angry, and can't respond in love. What is done to us in our present situation can be either real or perceived rejection; the pain is real to us either way. We all know Christians who are easily offended and respond in hurtful ways to others. That person needs inner healing so no one will inadvertently push their rejection button to trigger those wrong feelings and responses. When we are healed, our relationships are healed because we no longer hear everything through a filter of rejection.

There are also people we all know who have feelings of low self–worth and don't think very highly of themselves. An example would be that someone's parents were always be-littling them as a child so they don't walk in self–confidence. Low self–confidence would be the fruit we see, but the be-littling as a child is the root we don't see. In their adult life, whenever anything new is tried or they have to accomplish something, it triggers the pain of what happened to them as a child. They don't feel confident to do the task at hand even though they may actually accomplish it. Negative feelings hold them back from all that God has for them and prevent them from leaving their comfort zone. They may never understand that what they are feeling in the present, is rooted in their childhood. They never go beyond their comfort zone because they lack the self–confidence to do so. All of this stems from unhealed areas in their childhood. Inner healing will bring them into freedom from their low self–worth and lack of confi-dence.

Perhaps there is someone who was sexually abused in her

childhood and as an adult, experiences a crisis in her marriage. She has major trust issues triggered by her husband and can't seem to trust God either. She is not able to have intimacy with God or man, but there is help and healing for this woman to bring her peace, trust, and wholeness. Where she couldn't have healthy relationships, inner healing enables her to begin to respond to others without all her walls of self–protection and distrust. These walls have been removed and no longer keep her in an emotional prison. There have been many inner healing sessions with those who have been abused, where they were healed, made whole, and able to trust men and God for the first time in their lives.

There are so many more examples of the effects we can still have from our childhood, which have become hindrances in our adult lives and keep us from being able to fulfill the destiny written on our scrolls.

"Jesus asked the boy's father, 'How long has he been like this?'
'From childhood,' he answered."
Mark 9:21 (NIV)

Inner healing is following the negative fruit in a person's life to the root of where that pain began in childhood and asking Jesus to heal them.

When the triggers of wrong thinking, fear, anger, and unforgiveness are removed, we no longer respond the same way we always did in the past and that part of our life is transformed. Our soul begins to prosper in that very area where Jesus heals us!

Another important foundation of inner healing is:

"And you will know the truth, and the truth will make you free."

John 8:32 (NASB)

Jesus comes in with truth and makes us free to live in the fruit of the Spirit, found in Galatians 5:22–23, which are these wonderful attributes: *love, joy, peace, patience, kindness, goodness, faithfulness, gentleness, and self-control.* When we are walking in the fruit of the Spirit, we are able to live in the fullness of what was written on our scrolls. Jesus wants to remove *all* hindrances and obstacles to this destiny!

People need inner healing for many reasons:

- sins they can't overcome
- issues they struggle with emotionally
- problems in relationships
- chronic negative memories
- wrong responses in situations
- anger issues
- being critical and judgmental of others
- controlling behavior
- feeling they are a victim or full of self-pity
- rebellion and authority issues
- low self–worth/lack of confidence
- self–hatred
- rejection or being easily offended
- panic attacks or fear
- sexual, physical, and emotional abuse
- chronic depression
- growing up in a home with witchcraft or the occult
- and many more reasons

Lord, I declare those reading this book are beginning to understand they may have hindrances in their lives, and are beginning to realize there is hope and healing to transform them. Lead them to those who can minister inner healing to the roots of these wrong responses and hurtful ways they haven't been able to change. Illuminate the root to the negative fruit they have and replace *their* lies with *Your* truth.

In Jesus' name, Amen.

SOWING AND REAPING

There are physical laws as well as spiritual laws that operate, whether we understand them or not.

There are laws in the physical realm and there are also spiritual laws that operate *all* the time. The physical law of gravity was operating *long* before Newton observed the apple falling from the tree and discovered the law of gravity. It really doesn't matter that we may not understand or believe in the law of gravity, it will still operate anyway, *all* the time!

There are also spiritual laws in the Word of God, whether we know or believe they are there, that still operate like the law of gravity does in the physical realm.

"Do not be deceived, God is not mocked; for whatever a man sows, this he will also reap."
Galatians 6:7 (NASB)

What does it mean to sow and reap? It's a farming phrase that is used to help us understand how this law operates. We *sow* or plant seeds in the ground and when they are mature, we *reap* or bring in the harvest. If we plant eggplant seeds we will get mature eggplants and if we plant corn seeds we will get a harvest of corn. We can *never* plant peas which turn into tomatoes or plant squash and harvest peppers. Whatever we plant is what is produced and harvested.

What does this law have to do with us? This principle applies to everyone, whether they are a Christian or not, just like the principle of gravity. Sowing means – *everything* we *do* or *say* will reap a harvest in our life. If we sow to the good, we reap a good harvest and if we sow to the bad, we reap a bad harvest back into our lives. Whatever we sow, we will reap a harvest according to what was sown.

> *"Whoever sows injustice reaps calamity."*
> Proverbs 22:8a (NIV)

In this verse we see that if we sow injustice, then we reap the harvest of calamity. Calamity is *'a great misfortune or disaster, grievous affliction, adversity, and misery.'* There are always consequences to what is sown, whether good or bad. Injustice is a bad seed and will produce a bad harvest of calamity.

> *"The one who sows righteousness reaps a sure reward."*
> Proverbs 11:18b (NIV)

Here we see that if we sow righteousness, which means *'acting in accord with divine or moral law,'* then we reap a sure reward; something valuable is received. Righteousness is a good seed which produces a good harvest of a reward. We see this law of sowing and reaping both in the positive and negative realms *throughout* scripture.

Rest assured *whatever* we sow, we will also reap.

If we want a good harvest in our lives, we need to sow positive words and actions. If we sow love to others, we reap love from others. If we sow patience for others, we reap patience from others. If we sow generosity to others, we reap generosity from others, etc.

On the other hand, we could sow negative things to others and reap that harvest back instead. If we sow hatred toward others, we reap hatred. If we sow impatience, we reap impatience. If we are stingy with others, then we will reap stinginess.

This is a very *important* law to understand as we move into teaching inner healing.

We also saw this law of sowing and reaping demonstrated in the last chapter; if we don't forgive others for their sins, our sins won't be forgiven. The spiritual law of sowing and reaping is found throughout the Bible.

I am *not* trying to say, wounds that become pain in our lives are from something we have sown and we deserve it. Wounds come from imperfect people who do or say things that cause us pain and that pain becomes strongholds in our life. The great news is that Jesus came to free us from that pain!

Lord, I pray we see how the law of sowing and reaping has impacted our lives. I declare those things that are bringing negative fruit be exposed so we can replace them with the good fruit You desire we walk in. Transform our lives so we will have a harvest of peace, joy, and love in every area we sow.

In Jesus' name, Amen.

Chapter 4

WHERE DO WE BEGIN?

Where do we begin this inner healing process in a person's life?

When I first started in the inner healing ministry, the Lord gave me a vision of a large metal box with rivets on the corners. I heard Him say the box represented generational bondage in a person's life, which we shall explain in this chapter. It was made of the same metal as armored cars. He told me the reason that particular metal was used is because nothing can get in and nothing can get out. Because of this, they use this metal to protect what is put in the armored car. He also told me that this was a picture of the structure of a bondage in a person's generational bloodline. Until that box and its structure is dismantled through prayer, nothing will get in or out of that person's life. The Lord said we needed to *begin* ministry to people by dismantling generational bondages, these structures, in their family bloodline.

All bondages were put on the cross, as Jesus bore them all for us and paid the ultimate price by shedding His blood for them.

But there is something *we* need to do in order to be forgiven.

"If we say we have no sin, we deceive ourselves, and the truth is not in us. If we confess our sins, He is faithful and just to forgive us our sins and to cleanse us from all unrighteousness."
I John 1:8–9 (ESV)

**They stood to confess their sins and the
sins of their ancestors.**

Transformation healing sessions begin with confession and repentance of the generational bondages in our family line. Nehemiah 9:2 says, they stood in their places and *confessed their sins* and the *sins of their ancestors.* Also, Leviticus 26:40 says, they *confessed their sins* and the *sins of their ancestors.* Here we have the biblical precedents for breaking generational bondages from our lives.

We *begin* ministering inner healing with the breaking of these generational bondages, but there will be *many* other obstacles we will discover, that must also be addressed.

So what are these generational bondages?

Generational Bondages

Romans 5:12 tells us that sin came from one man and now we *all* sin. Because we were all born from Adam, we were born with sin that has tainted our lives and caused hurt, pain, and brokenness stemming from our past generations and families.

**We were born to imperfect parents who brought
us up to the best of their ability.**

Whether they were great parents or ones who were wounded themselves, and in turn ended up wounding their children, they were *all* imperfect so we need inner healing.

> *"The LORD is longsuffering, and of great mercy, forgiving iniquity and transgression, and by no means clearing the guilty, visiting the iniquity of the fathers upon the children unto the third and fourth generation."*
> Numbers 14:18 (KJV)

This scripture says there are generational iniquities or bondages, which means, *'the state of being bound by a compulsion,'* that are now passed onto our children to the third and fourth generation. When the fourth generation's children commit the same iniquities, they *continue* as bondages, and are passed on to three or four more generations. These bondages continue through our generational bloodlines until this pattern of sin is stopped.

Some people may say this isn't needed as Jesus paid for all of this on the cross and *yes,* He did. He died for the entire world, but in Romans 10:9–10, we are told that we still need to believe in Him to appropriate what He did for us. The word says, by His stripes we *are* healed, but so many Christians are still sick. It says of Jesus, in Matthew 4:23, that He healed *all* their diseases, so we need to appropriate what is freely ours. The bottom line is, we need to *appropriate* what Jesus did on the cross for us. If Jesus paid for all of this at the cross so it no longer affects us, then why do we see so many Christians who have physical and emotional issues? This is why God raises up healing ministries, because His people are harassed and helpless with no one to help them.

We all see many children of alcoholic parents who hated

what their parents were doing, but in turn grew up to become an alcoholic themselves. There are also children whose father abused their mother and then some sons grew up to abuse their wives, even though they hated what their father did to their mother. If they were a daughter, they may marry abusive men and repeat that pattern in their own life. These patterns are repeated because iniquities are passed through our blood-line and continue to manifest in future generations.

These iniquities cause all kinds of problems in families and the church through offenses, divisiveness, church splits, jeal-ousy, anger, authority issues, control, gossip, hatred, self–promotion, and so much more. Many wounded people go from church to church carrying their wounds and affecting the next place. But it doesn't have to stay that way!

I grew up hearing stories about an uncle who was a drug addict/alcoholic and would break into my grandmother's home to steal money and goods in order to support his habit. Before my aunt left him because of the addictions, they had a son. The son didn't grow up living with his father, but when he became a teenager, he started doing drugs and alcohol and broke into my grandmother's home to support his habit. For years, I was so puzzled in trying to figure out how a son could have done exactly what his father did when he didn't grow up with him. It certainly wasn't learned behavior, but it wasn't until I read the Bible verse in Numbers about the iniquity of the fathers being visited upon the children that I finally knew the answer. That bondage was passed on to his son through his bloodline.

Some examples of other bondages that follow and operate in family lines:

- anger, hatred, and murder

- jealousy and envy
- divorce
- rejection, bitterness, and unforgiveness
- adultery and other sexual sins
- fear, anxiety, and stress
- worry
- lying or stealing
- rebellion
- racism
- low self–worth/lack of confidence
- guilt, condemnation, and shame
- so much more

We may see some of these things in ourselves, our parents, grandparents, siblings, cousins, aunts, or uncles.

Begin by making a list of all the sins you are aware of in both your father's and mother's family, including yourself, your parents, siblings, grandparents, aunts, uncles, and cousins. Consider only those of your direct bloodline and not an aunt who is married to your father's brother. Depend on the Holy Spirit to show you what needs to be added to that list. Once you have made the list, pray through it using the prayer model on the next page.

There is a complete list of *all* the different categories of generational bondages available in our companion book *Designed for Destiny – Guide,* to help you with not only *this* but so much more.

We confess them on behalf of our family, and because they are part of our DNA bloodline, we confess them as our own, even if we haven't personally committed them. They still come through us and are passed on to our children who pass them to their children until the bondages are broken.

If there are more to be confessed later, ask the Holy Spirit to uncover any that are still affecting your life. When the Lord shows you more generational bondages, you can also pray to break *them* using this prayer model.

After confession and repentance, the last part of 1 John 9 says that *"God is faithful to forgive us our sins and cleanse us from all unrighteousness."* So once we break the bondages in our family line through repentance, we are now cleansed from all the un-righteousness that went before us.

Any adult children we have should do this for themselves.

The great news in Deuteronomy 7:9 is, once the bondages are broken and we love God and keep his commandments, He bestows His blessings to a thousand of our generations.

Emotional feelings may or may not follow the removal of bondages. Some people may have a sense of a weight being lifted from them, but others may not. Mark 11:24 says that whatever we ask for in prayer, believe we have received it, and it will be ours. We pray in faith and believe the bondages are broken.

Prayer for Generational Bondages

I confess the sins of my past generations and whatever they did to open the door to _____ (list them) in our family line. I confess them as my own and on behalf of my children and grandchildren (if you have them).

I take the sword of the Spirit, which is the Word of God, and cut the generational bondages from myself, all the way back through my past generations to Adam; and from myself through my children to future generations, forward to Jesus' return.

By faith, I take the cut ends of these sins and dip them in the blood of Jesus and declare, from this day forward, they shall never be put back together again.

I break all demonic structures and cancel all the sowing and reaping that has been in my family line because of these sins.

I declare, my bloodline is now cleansed and forgiven from the bondages I have confessed.

In Jesus' name, Amen...

Generational Illnesses

When we go to a doctor for the first time, they ask us to fill out a form for our medical history to list what diseases run in our family. It's because science has proven these illnesses are hereditary and passed on through our generational bloodline. We may see cancer, heart disease, diabetes, high blood pressure, high cholesterol, arthritis, many autoimmune diseases, and other illnesses that run in family lines.

That's why doctors ask for your medical history and some physicians may also ask if these illnesses were from your paternal or maternal side. Science has also proven many of these illnessses are caused by stress, as well as other family bondages like bitterness, fear, self-rejection, and more.

Deuteronomy 28 tells us what will happen to us for our

wrongdoing. It says in verse 21 that we will *have disease after disease following us*. We can look in our own family and trace many diseases and illnesses, thus breaking them in our family line through healing prayer. Stop and make a list of illnesses that run in your bloodline from both sides of your family before praying to break them.

Prayer for Generational Illnesses

I confess the sins of my past generations and whatever they did to open the door to _____ (list the illnesses) in our family line. I confess them as my own and on behalf of my children and grandchildren (if you have them).

I take the sword of the Spirit, which is the Word of God, and cut the generational illnesses from myself, all the way back through my past generations to Adam; and from myself through my children to future generations, forward to Jesus' return.

By faith, I take the cut ends of these diseases and dip them in the blood of Jesus and declare, from this day forward, they shall never be put back together again.

I break all demonic structures and cancel all the sowing and reaping that has been in my family line because of these illnesses.

I declare, my bloodline is now cleansed and forgiven from the illness bondages I have confessed.

In Jesus' name, Amen...

Generational Occult

"Cursed is the man who makes an idol or a molten image,
an abomination to the LORD, the work of the hands of
the craftsman, and sets it up in <u>secret</u>."
Deuteronomy 27:15 (NASB)

The word occult comes from the Latin word meaning *'hidden or secret.'*

We become cursed if we practice idolatry, which is worshipping other gods instead of the one true God. This verse also says, what they do is done in secret and not in the open for everyone to see. This goes back to the meaning of the word occult: *'hidden.'* The occult is: secret, hidden practices that come from the supernatural realm of demonic darkness. If we or someone in our generational line have practiced the occult, like witchcraft or other demonic art such as superstitions, eastern religions, horoscopes, rituals, Ouija boards, 8 balls, Masonic rites, New Age or levitation games (to name a few), it opens the door for those sins and the spiritual effects to be passed on to the children to the third and fourth generation.

The effects of those past generational occult rituals and practices are still operating in our generational lines until broken. These practices may cause unexplainable trauma, torment, mental or physical illnesses, early death, or turmoil in family lines, and will follow that family line until broken and cleansed.

Stop and make a list of all known occult practices, *or* ones the Holy Spirit reveals to you, before praying to break them in your bloodline.

Prayer for Generational Occult Practices

I confess the sins of my past generations and whatever they did to open the door to _____ (list the occult activity) in our family line. I confess them as my own and on behalf of my children and grandchildren (if you have them).

I take the sword of the Spirit, which is the Word of God, and cut the generational occult bondages from myself, all the way back through my past generations to Adam; and from myself through my children to future generations, forward to Jesus' return.

By faith, I take the cut ends of these occult practices and dip them in the blood of Jesus and declare, from this day forward, they shall never be put back together again.

I break all demonic structures, rituals, dedications, sacrifices, spells, curses, and also cancel all the sowing and reaping that has been in my family line because of this occult involvement.

I declare, my bloodline is now cleansed and forgiven from the occult bondages I have confessed.

I close the spiritual door opened by these occult practices and declare it shall never be opened again.

In Jesus' name, Amen.

We have now appropriated what Jesus did on the cross for us through repentance on behalf of our generations for sins, diseases, and occult practices.

Chapter 5

SOUL TIES

"As soon as he had finished speaking to Saul, the <u>soul</u> of Jonathan <u>was</u> <u>knit</u> <u>to</u> <u>the</u> <u>soul</u> of David, and Jonathan loved him as his own soul."
I Samuel 18:1 (ESV)

The soul of Jonathan was knit to the soul of David, forming a soul tie.

We see from this verse how the soul of Jonathan was knit to the soul of David and Jonathan loved him as his own soul. This is what has been termed a *soul tie,* and is a picture of a godly soul tie.

We have godly soul ties with our parents, spouse, family, friends, other Christians, etc., and they are healthy and good. We have been created to have godly soul ties of love, friendship, and intimacy with those we are in close relationship with.

UNGODLY SOUL TIES

But what happens if we have soul ties with others that are not healthy? What if we were in a codependent relationship with someone like our spouse, parent, friend, or teacher? Codependency is defined as *'excessive emotional or psychological reliance on someone.'* A picture of classic codependency is the alcoholic husband and his enabling wife.

It can also occur in a relationship between a mother who has lost her husband and a son who becomes the man of the house, taking his father's place. I'm familiar with a situation where a man's father died when he was 10 years old and as the oldest son, he became the man of the house. He married but was still attached to his mother and put her before his wife. The wife became very resentful because her husband would frequently call or visit his mother, causing the wife to feel her mother–in–law's desires were more important than her own. She always felt second place to his mom and tried to reach him with that truth until it became a crisis in their marriage.

Our ungodly soul ties prevent us from developing and maintaining healthy, godly relationships and may eventually become harmful. What do we do about soul ties that are ungodly? We pray to break them out of our lives. A son is never meant to take the *place* of his father, so that relationship became codependent, unhealthy, and ungodly. Naturally a son will help his mom, but should not *spiritually* take the father's place. This man stepped out of his godly soul tie with his mom, into an ungodly and codependent soul tie.

There may also be a student who has an ungodly soul tie with their teacher. This can happen when the teacher allows the student to become too familiar with their personal information or issues. The relationship may not only be ungodly, but may even lead to sexual expression.

A woman may develop an ungodly soul tie with a coworker when she has all of her emotional needs met by the coworker instead of her husband. It's possible for a pastor to develop a soul tie when counseling a woman who becomes overly dependent on him.

There are codependent wives who are abused by their husbands, or whose husbands are alcoholics, who stay in the home but never confront the issues; this enables their husbands to stay broken.

We may also form an ungodly soul tie with someone we *depend* on for our spiritual needs. We depend on *them* for our answers and help, in place of God. There is a time for obtaining spiritual counsel and prayer from others, but this goes beyond that into a codependent relationship.

When we have painful, dysfunctional relationships with our parents or spouse, we may form unhealthy soul ties with them that need to be broken. This is very important to our healing process so we are able to have the healthy, godly soul ties that the Lord intended we have with them.

There are so many more examples we could share of ungodly, codependent soul ties that need to be broken.

In that case of the man who appeared to value his mother more than his wife, he didn't realize he had an ungodly soul tie with his mother. Although he didn't see it in himself, he was willing to pray for the ungodly soul tie to be broken if it would help the relationship with his wife. He prayed to break the soul tie and the husband said that he actually felt it break off and his heart unite with his wife. From that point on, the wife became first in their marriage. We read in Matthew 19:5, that *"a man shall leave his father and mother and be united to his wife."* This husband finally left his mother through the breaking of that ungodly soul tie and became united to his wife. Now he had a *godly* soul tie with his mother and he could enjoy the natural mother/son relationship that God intended. The wife saw such a huge difference in their relationship and actually felt loved. She finally had the place a wife should have in her husband's life.

Ask the Holy Spirit to reveal to you if you have any ungodly soul ties with others and then pray this prayer.

Prayer for Ungodly Soul Ties

Lord, forgive me for walking in a codependent relationship with _____ (name them). I now realize this is an ungodly and unhealthy soul tie I have with them.

I forgive _____ for everything (he/she) has done in this codependent relationship and I no longer hold (him/her) accountable for (his/her) sins.

Forgive me for walking in an unhealthy relationship with this person.

I take the sword of the Spirit and break this soul tie from my life and come out of agreement with the codependency I have been walking in with (him/her).

I also break all the sowing and reaping this codependent relationship has brought into my life.

Thank You, Lord, from this day forth, I can now walk in a godly and healthy soul tie with them and be able to do what *You* lead me to do in this relationship.

In the name of Jesus, Amen!

SEXUAL SOUL TIES

Below we see a *godly* soul tie in a sexual union between a husband and wife, where they are now united and the two become one flesh.

For this reason a man will leave his father and mother and be united to his wife, and the two will become one flesh. So they are no longer two, but one flesh.
Matthew 19:5–6a (BSB)

There is another kind of *ungodly* soul tie we enter into when we have a sexual union with someone other than our spouse.

"Do you not know your bodies are members of Christ? Shall I then take away the members of Christ and make them members of a prostitute? May it never be! Or do you not know that the one who joins himself to a prostitute is one body with her? For He says, 'The two shall become one flesh.'"
I Corinthians 6:15–16 (ESV)

Both verses say the two become one flesh, but one refers to a godly sexual union and the other to an ungodly, as it says, "*may it never be,*" in the joining of a sexual union between a man with someone who isn't his wife. There is an explanation from the verse in Matthew saying, they are no longer two but one flesh. This signifies not only the picture of what happens when the two come together in the physical sense, but also the spiritual aspect of what happens when they consummate that oneness.

After a sexual union, we become and remain united, as one body and one flesh with that person.

Why would the Bible say that joining oneself to a prostitute makes us a member of that prostitute? What is meant by the term *becoming one flesh* besides the physical aspect? It's because our souls, which comprise our mind, will, and emotions, become connected to one another. It creates a spiritual soul tie where one person's soul is tied to the other person's soul, and now they've become and remain *one flesh* with that person.

Matthew 5:28 says, *if we lust after a woman, we have committed adultery with her in our heart.* So we also have an emotional soul tie with everyone we've ever lusted after. This is why pornography is dangerous, as a soul tie is created with those we don't even know.

Sexually intimate persons are connected spiritually in the soulish realm to one another. This one flesh would not be spoken about in the Bible if that one flesh wasn't also spiritually significant. There wouldn't be warnings about becoming one with prostitutes if that wasn't spiritually significant. The truth is, we are spiritually united as one flesh with them.

The problem is, this is exactly what happens when we have sex with people other than our spouse. If we have multiple partners before marriage, those people are *permanently* united with us. We have become *one flesh* with them, and God meant for us to become one flesh with only one person, our spouse.

Because we have oneness with others, it interferes with our ability to *truly* be one with our spouse.

Sexual intimacy outside of marriage brings spiritual and emotional confusion in our marriages and causes problems. Sometimes women and men can't seem to get prior relationships out of their minds and hearts, even though they are married to someone else.

Sexual soul ties with all of those other partners must be broken. This alleviates the *interference* and *confusion* which comes from all of those with whom we became one flesh prior to being married.

The same cleansing applies to adultery, which is sexual intimacy with someone other than our spouse while married. When we remove those sexual soul ties, we can be truly united with our spouse. If not married, then we become pure in preparation for a future spouse. If we are divorced from our spouse, we would also need to break that soul tie with them.

In some instances, people may actually feel the ties with prior partners break.

Please list the names of those past sexual relationships you have had and then use the prayer model below to break those soul ties. If you don't remember their names, you can still break them. This list is for your private use in prayer and may be shredded after the soul ties have been broken.

Prayer for Sexual Soul Ties

Lord, forgive me for having sex outside of marriage with _____ (name them). I now realize this is an ungodly and unhealthy soul tie because I have become one flesh with them and have united myself to them, physically and spiritually, by the sexual union we had.

I take the sword of the Spirit and break this soul tie from my life, and also break the one flesh it has produced between us.

I forgive them for everything they have done in this relationship and no longer hold them accountable for their sins against me. Also, please forgive me for all the things I may have done to them during our relationship.

I break all the sowing and reaping this *one flesh* relationship has brought into my life.

Thank You, Lord, from this day forth, I am now one with my spouse and we truly have become one flesh.

Or if single….

Isaiah 54:5 *(ESV) "The Maker is your husband, The Lord Almighty is His name."*

In Jesus' name, Amen!

Chapter 6

VOWS AND CURSES

INNER VOWS

Inner vow means: *'a person's solemn declaration that he or she will do or not do a specific thing.'* Synonyms of vow: *'oath, pledge, and promise.'* Secondary meanings are: *'agreement, compact, contract, covenant, and guarantee.'*

> *"For as he (man) thinks in his heart, so is he."*
> Proverbs 23:7a (NKJV)

We often make inner vows early in our life as the result of pain we experience and set them in place for our self–protection. We simply don't realize the impact they continue to have in our adult lives. Though long forgotten, they still have the power to keep us from walking in freedom. Having forgotten all about making an oath doesn't discount the fact that it is still operating in our adult life. The spiritual law of sowing and reaping is still operating even though we don't remember the inner vow is there. We have entered into a prison of our own making and the truth is, we never grow out of these inner vows. In inner healing, we find a lot of people who made inner vows and when they are broken, there is such freedom and transformation that comes.

An *inner vow* is something we set in our mind and heart to protect us from future pain.

It becomes a promise we make to ourselves and often involves the use of words like *always* and *never*. Inner vows are made in response to emotional pain, hurts, expectations, or needs that weren't met. They are actually oaths we made and their power continues to operate until they are recognized and broken.

Time never changes the power of our oath, but only causes us to forget it's even there. We know we shouldn't feel or think a certain way, but fail to realize it's because we made an inner vow earlier in our life. We never grow out of these vows until they are revealed and we come out of agreement with them. Herein lies the problem, once we come into agreement with those words, we fulfill them. They are now a *permanent* part of our thinking and response process, buried in our subconscious mind, following us throughout our existence, and causing such hindrances to our happiness and peace.

Again, it's one of those spiritual laws that operates in Proverbs 23:7 that we are what we think, even when we don't understand it's buried in our subconscious mind and still affecting us.

The effect of an inner vow is two–fold. First, it was made to protect us from future pain, and second, it is a bitter root judgment made against the person who caused that pain. A bitter root happens when we become offended and walk in unforgiveness toward the one who caused the pain, and now judge them. What we don't realize is when we judge others and make an inner vow, we enter into the law of sowing and reaping again. We don't understand how important this spiritual law becomes in our lives or how the law is activated. Here is the sowing and reaping law about judging others.

"Do not judge, or you too will be judged. For in the same way you judge others, you will be judged, and with the measure you use, it will be measured to you."
Matthew 7:1-2 (NIV)

It's crucial to break any inner vows we have made. Let's look at some examples of inner vows and how they affect our lives.

A child may experience a deep hurt or wound inflicted by someone close or significant to them. Their response may be to make an inner vow, *"I will never let anyone get close to me again!"* When they become an adult, they have forgotten all about making this inner vow, but it will be the root cause of major intimacy issues with everyone: their spouse, children, family members, friends, and even God. They desperately want to have loving and close relationships, but somehow can never achieve them and wonder what's wrong. This oath may have been made when they were eight years old, but still has the power to *"never let anyone get close to me again."* During the inner healing process, this inner vow is revealed.

When an inner vow is broken and the person who hurt us is forgiven, our life is dramatically changed. Where we could not feel close to anyone in the past, we begin to be able to feel close to others and God for the first time. This is a process leading to freedom and wholeness.

Some people have made *many* inner vows because they grew

up in highly dysfunctional homes, but so many of us make them even if our childhood seemed ideal.

We make inner vows early in our life which keep us from walking in maturity in that *specific* area.

These oaths also prevent us from being able to walk in all that God has written for us in our book in heaven.

For example, a man grew up not being able to please his angry dad who was harsh with his son's mistakes and faults. At some point in his young life, the son made the oath, "*I am a failure and can't do anything right!*" He grew up, got a college degree, a great job, wife, and children. But no matter what he did or said, he felt like such a failure in his job, as a husband, as a father, and in whatever he did for the Lord. He couldn't get beyond those feelings and truly *believed* he was a failure. Early in his childhood, he came into agreement with those harsh words from his dad. The statements were now *long* forgotten, but still had such absolute power in his adulthood. The results of his oath was also interfering with his relationship with God because he saw God as that angry Dad who was harsh because of His son's faults and mistakes. He *knew* the truth but was unable to walk in that truth. He sought inner healing because he was so tired of feeling like a failure.

During the inner healing process, the Holy Spirit revealed that inner vow he made; it was broken and the man came out of agreement with those words. He also forgave his dad and repented for judging him. For the first time in his life, this man no longer feels like a failure and can now walk in freedom and wholeness. His relationship with God was healed as well, and he no longer saw Him through that harsh father filter.

We *all* walk in lies which keep us in an emotional prison, but the great news is that Jesus wants to replace all our lies with His truth that sets us free.

In another scenario, a woman may have had a very difficult childhood and makes a vow early in her life, "*Growing up is too difficult, so I will never grow up.*" As an adult, she becomes very immature and irresponsible, which causes problems in her marriage and with her children. She wants help but isn't aware of the root cause of her problems. During the inner healing process, Jesus highlights the inner vow she made. She breaks the vow, comes out of agreement with it, forgives her parents, and repents for judging them. The woman becomes free and can begin the maturing process for the first time in her life, because she finally has given herself permission to grow up. She can start a whole new life!

What are some examples of inner vows we can make?

- If I am perfect, then others will accept me.
- If others find out who I really am, they will never accept me.
- I will never trust anyone.
- I will never let another man hurt me again.
- It's always my fault.
- I am the only one who can protect me.
- I am stupid or a failure.
- People always reject me.
- I will never be dependent on others again.
- I don't need anyone.
- No one ever listens to me.
- No matter what I say, it won't change anything.
- Nothing ever goes right in my life.
- I will never be like my mother/father.

- Authority figures always hurt me.
- plus so many other inner vows we may make....

Take a moment and allow the Holy Spirit to search your heart and see if any inner vows are highlighted to *you*. Jesus wants to break the power of those words in your life. Write them down and pray this prayer for each one of them revealed to you.

Prayer for Inner Vows

Forgive me Lord for making the inner vow _____ (name it). I now understand I've created a prison of my own making and it still has power in my life to keep me bound in that area. I don't want to live in this prison any longer and choose to step out into freedom.

I forgive _____ for hurting me and also, please forgive me for judging them.

I take the sword of the Spirit and break the power of this inner vow from my life and come out of agreement with these words.

I remove all the negative sowing and reaping that has occurred since I made that oath. It no longer has any power from this moment forth.

I thank You, Lord, that _____ (now speak the truth which is the opposite of the inner vow).

Also, forgive me for how this has interfered with my relationship with You and for seeing You through the filter of this inner vow.

In Jesus' name, Amen!

WORD CURSES

*"With the tongue we bless our Lord and Father, and with it <u>we</u> <u>curse</u> <u>men</u>, who have been made in God's likeness.
<u>Out</u> <u>of</u> <u>the</u> <u>same</u> <u>mouth</u> <u>come</u> <u>blessing</u> <u>and</u> <u>cursing</u>.
My brothers, this should not be!"*
James 3:9-10 (BSB)

From our own mouth comes both blessings and curses and it specifically says that with our tongue we can curse men. These curses operate *exactly* the same as inner vows, only they are spoken by *others* about us at a very early age. As a child, we believe *everything* people say to us before we grow older and come to understand that not everything spoken about us is true.

**We receive them, believe them, and come
into agreement with those words.**

Word curses hold the same power that inner vows do. They have no expiration date and will continue to operate through the spiritual law of Proverbs 23 that says, *"As a man thinks in his heart, so he is."* These word curses become the filter through which we see and hear *everything*.

The enemy is quick to reinforce these words to keep us in an emotional prison, which prevents us from moving forward in our Christian walk.

I know a woman whose mother always told her, *"No one will ever put up with you."* This became a word curse and she grew up believing that if anyone found out who she really was, they would reject her and leave. This woman married the first man who asked her; she was afraid if she didn't accept, no one would ever ask her again. Everything was heard through this filter of rejection and caused her pain. She became angry and lashed out at those she felt rejected her. The woman needed inner healing from so many issues, including breaking this word curse spoken by her mother and forgiving her for it.

There was also a man whose father insulted him throughout his early years. When the son didn't do things the way the father expected, he would hear, *"What are you, an idiot?"* This boy hated school and believed he was stupid, an idiot. At the age of 15 he was skipping school and at 16, he quit high school. His teachers told the parents they couldn't figure out why, because he was so smart. He ended up getting his GED and tried college, but quit after the first semester because he felt he couldn't do the work. It was very crippling to this man and he needed to break that word curse over himself and forgive his father for it.

"Death and life are in the power of the tongue, and those who love it will eat its fruit."
Proverbs 18:21 (NIV)

Our life is *dramatically* transformed after the word curses are broken and the lies are removed! We have seen this time and time again in so many lives, where there is no more power in those inner vows and word curses and such freedom comes.

Here is a brief list of possible word curses that could be spoken by parents, siblings, teachers, peers, etc.

- You will never amount to anything.
- You are terrible in _____ (math).
- Children should be seen and not heard.
- Why can't you be more like your _____ (sister)?
- You are always sick.
- You can't do anything right.
- You don't get along with anyone.
- You'd better lose weight or others won't accept you.
- Your grades leave a lot to be desired.
- What's wrong with you?
- You are so disobedient.
- You are stupid.
- Things bullies would say to us in school like: 'no one likes you,' 'you're so ugly,' 'you don't fit in with us,' 'you're a nerd,' and so many other terrible things.

Maybe one of these word curses struck a nerve with you or triggered some other curses that came to mind. Stop here and ask the Holy Spirit to reveal to you any word curses He wants to break. You may have forgotten them but they have come to mind and are still keeping you captive today. Write them down before praying.

Prayer for Word Curses

Forgive me Lord for receiving the word curse _____ (name it). I now understand this created a prison of my own making and still has power to keep me bound in that area. I don't want to live in this prison any longer and choose to step out into freedom.

I forgive _____ for speaking this word curse.

I break the power of this word curse and take the sword of the Spirit and cut it from my life. I also come out of agreement with these words that have been spoken.

I cancel all the negative sowing and reaping that has occurred since I came into agreement with this word curse. It no longer has any power from this moment forth.

I thank You Lord that _____ (now speak the truth which is the opposite of the word curse).

Also, forgive me for how this has interfered with my relationship with You and for seeing You through the filter of this word curse.

In Jesus' name, Amen.

Most inner vows and word curses are revealed when the inner healing of struggles and triggers come up in our lives as the Holy Spirit ministers to set us free.

Chapter 7

IMAGINATIONS AND MEMORIES

IMAGINATIONS

I want to begin by dispelling some misconceptions people have about the imagination. God has given us an imagination which we can use for either good or evil. Before Adam and Eve fell, our imagination was pure and used for the Glory of God. Genesis 1:27 says that God *"created mankind in his own image, in the image of God he created them; male and female he created them."* God has an imagination and He gave us one as we were created in His image.

God created us in His image and gave us our imagination so it is *good*!

God imagined the earth and created it, as well as the stars and put them into place. He envisioned the beautifully colored flowers and the blue sky and *whatever* He imagined came to be.

Satan caused Adam and Eve to fall and now our imaginations

have the capacity for evil as well as good. Besides imagining what our baby will grow up to be, what our life career might be, or how to create a project, our imaginations can also come up with a way to murder someone, commit adultery, or plan a bank heist, all before anything is acted upon. The word says in James 1:14–15 that sin is conceived in the mind and then gives birth to our actions.

The mind is not *only* our intellect but also includes our imagination. As we envision what something would look or feel like and dwell on it, we can act upon those imaginings. Like God, Who imagined the earth and acted upon His concept. We can also choose to use our imagination for sin instead of the good for which it was originally created.

Artists, musicians, architects, and so many others use this God–given gift of imagination to create wonderful works that are beneficial to man and glorify God. Or, they can use these same creative powers to create things that don't honor God, to be used for evil purposes.

The supernatural realm of God was His original intent for our imagination. But Satan came up with a plan to use fear to keep us from using our imagination for the Lord's purposes in the supernatural realm. Satan counterfeits *everything* the Lord has given man and uses it for *his* own purposes. New Age is one of those purposes, which uses people's imagination for the occult. They use the imagination to tap into the powers of darkness and because of the occult, many Christians have now become afraid to use their imagination for the supernatural realm of God. Satan has stolen from us that which rightfully belongs to us and now keeps us in fear. We may walk in spiritual gifts but because of fear, some have rejected using their imagination *fully* as God originally intended. They fear Satan will somehow deceive them and it will open the door to the demonic realm. Satan is *delighted* when he succeeds in keeping us from our rightful use of the imagination.

Actually, we *do* use our imagination every day. We may remember something wonderful that happened with someone we love, such as a romantic dinner, and live it again in our imagination. Something we see, feel, or smell can bring us back to a wonderful memory we can live again in our imagination. We can imagine a beautiful field of flowers or a dream in our heart and imagine what it would be like to follow that wonderful dream. We use our imagination every day, yet many people still discount using it for the Kingdom of God and His supernatural realm.

Some, because of those who have used it for the dark supernatural realm and occult, now may become fearful it will take them into darkness. I say, it's time to take it back for the Kingdom of God and His use!

Dr. Dale Fife wrote in his book *The Imagination Master* that he heard God tell him,

"The imagination is the page I write on."

When the Lord gives us a vision, more often than not, it happens in our imagination. The Bible tells us in Acts 2:17 that *"your young men will see visions and your old men will dream dreams."* Dreams also happen in our imagination, whether dreams from God or our own. Many have had dreams from the Lord giving warnings, instructions, or callings, and these dreams take place in our imagination.

It is time to take back what Satan has stolen and begin to allow the Holy Spirit, once again, access to our imagination to begin seeing all the wonderful things God has in store for us in heavenly realms.

Remember, our imagination was given to us by God to be used for His purposes and *we* choose to use it for good or evil.

"What father among you, if his son asks for a fish, will give him a snake instead? Or if he asks for an egg, will give him a scorpion? Therefore if you, being evil, know to give good gifts to your children, how much more will the Father who is in heaven give the Holy Spirit to those asking Him!"
Luke 11:11-13 (BSB)

Instead of walking in fear that *somehow* Satan will use our imagination for his purpose and lead us into darkness, *believe* that if we ask God for a fish, He won't give us a snake. His word is absolute truth and we can depend on what He says! This means God will give us the Holy Spirit when we ask *Him* to use our imaginations for His Kingdom purposes and this should cancel out any fear. We can be *absolutely assured* by this verse, the Holy Spirit *won't* lead us into darkness.

MEMORIES

During the ministry of inner healing of memories, the imagination is activated by Jesus to bring healing and freedom from the pain and lies of our past through the memories the Holy Spirit brings into our mind.

"Forget the former things; <u>do not dwell on the past</u>. See I am doing a new thing! Now it springs up; do you not perceive it? I am making a way in the desert and streams in the wasteland."

Isaiah 43:18–19 (NIV)

If we are commanded to forget the former things and not to dwell on the past, then we need to have a *way* to get *beyond* the former things that happened in our past. In inner healing, Jesus is doing a new thing by 'making a way in our desert and bringing streams to our wastelands'. What do deserts and wastelands represent in inner healing? They are symbolic of those things from the past that keep us bound in pain and trigger wrong responses, feelings, and thoughts. Jesus wants to come in and do a new thing in that painful memory. He wants to remove the *lies* that have bound us and replace them with *His truth*. When we are no longer walking in lies, we walk further and deeper into our destiny. Jesus accomplishes this by healing painful memories.

God loves us so much, He has provided healing for our soul so it can begin to prosper, which releases us further into His plans and destiny for our life. How awesome is that?

I remember meeting a woman in need of inner healing from abuse. She told us she had already forgiven her abusive father, and asked why she needed to do go through inner healing. When I asked the Holy Spirit how to reply, He said; *"She may have forgiven her father, but now I want to heal the pain he caused that is keeping her from being everything I created her to be."* There were still deserts and wastelands in her life God wanted to make into living streams. She went on to receive inner healing for the abuse, was transformed, and became a believer in the healing of memories.

"When I was a child, I talked like a child, I thought like a child, I reasoned like a child. When I became a man, I put the ways of childhood behind me."

I Corinthians 13:11 (NIV)

We can look around the church and see adults that still talk like a child, think like a child, and reason like a child.

Those people became chronological adults, but they never put their childish ways behind them. They have become locked in an emotional prison because of painful memories that still affect who they are today in how they think, act, and respond to people and life's circumstances. This stems from childhood memories that have lied to them about who they are. They have become stuck in those lies, and are unable to walk in the destiny that is written in their book.

Children don't have the ability to rationalize and come up with adult conclusions to complicated situations. *Everything* in their little lives has to have an explanation. So they fill the gaps in their understanding with explanations from their young perspective and thinking. In those painful circumstances, their childish explanations are not based on adult perspectives, but on lies they saw as truth. Satan, according to John 8:44, is the father of lies; he feeds them *false information* about the situation and now this perceived truth is still operating in their adult lives. This is *exposed* and *healed* during the healing of memories.

We all have areas in our lives where we have wrong responses that originate from unhealed areas and the lies we have believed since childhood. The truth is, there are many people in the body of Christ who still respond and act in ways that are not Christlike, even though they belong to Jesus and have Him living in them. They are depressed, constantly offended, oppressed, extremely negative, aggressive toward the pastor and others, walking in anger and jealousy, unable to submit to authority, and so much more. The good news is that Jesus loves us too much to leave us in that state.

Most of us have more than one issue requiring healing. Our prominent daily struggles and challenges reveal the roots our Lord wishes to address.

Lord, I declare that people are seeing the truth about the use of their imagination and memories to bring inner healing to their lives. I declare the enemy can no longer cause fear and misunderstanding, in order to rob us from using our imagination for *any* godly spiritual use in the Kingdom of God and for His purposes.

In Jesus' name, Amen.

ALL THE DAYS ORDAINED FOR ME
WERE WRITTEN IN YOUR BOOK BEFORE
ONE OF THEM CAME TO BE.
PSALM 139:16 (NIV)

Chapter 8

HEALING OF MEMORIES

People may not understand how the Lord uses our imagination to do the healing. The Holy Spirit uses the avenue of our imagination by bringing to us the painful memory for the *sole* purpose of healing and freedom. Remember, if we ask God to have Jesus go into our memory to bring us back to where it all began, *He won't* lead us into darkness. We must not allow fear to capture us as God can *always* be trusted not to give us a scorpion when we are asking for an egg. The Lord will *never* give us something bad if we are asking Him for a good thing. It is actually Satan who doesn't want us healed and will lie to us to keep us in fear, so we won't receive the healing we desperately need for our freedom and wholeness.

The Lord uses our imagination for the healing so we can see or sense Jesus in that memory *He* brought to our imagination. What *Jesus* shows us or speaks to us *heals* that painful memory. He replaces *all the lies* holding us captive with His *truth* that sets us free.

Others may also want to know where this type of ministry is found in the Bible, so I asked the Lord to show me what He had to say about the healing of memories. He answered by quoting this verse to me:

"Likewise, every good tree bears good fruit, but a bad tree bears bad fruit. A good tree cannot bear bad fruit, and a bad tree cannot bear good fruit."
Matthew 7:17-18 (BSB)

The Lord asked me to look at the fruit that has come from the healing of memories. As I reflected, I saw the numerous lives that have been transformed and set free. I recalled many people who had been in years of counseling, but were set free in a few sessions by the Holy Spirit's guidance. The Lord told me this kind of good fruit can only come from a good tree, as a bad tree could *never* produce the good fruit we are seeing in people's lives. I believed Him and His answer in this scripture He gave me, and it's settled in my heart.

"He reveals the deep things of darkness and brings deep shadows into the light."
Job 12:22 (NET)

The Holy Spirit is the one who reveals the painful memories buried in our subconscious mind (deep things of darkness) and brings them, for our freedom and transformation, into the light for healing.

"Send forth your light and your truth, let them guide me."
Psalm 43:3a (NLT)

This verse is a great picture of what Jesus does in the healing of memories. He sends light by the Holy Spirit to lead us out of lies into His truth. He guides the session the entire time, from the memories that come into our imagination, all the way to the healing and transformation *He* accomplishes in our life through the healing of those memories.

"You are the God who performs miracles."
Psalm 77:14 (NIV)

What the Lord does to set the captives free and to replace our darkness with His light, during the healing of memories, is nothing short of miraculous.

"Trust in the Lord with all your heart and lean not on your own understanding; in all your ways acknowledge Him, and He will make your paths straight."
Prov. 3:5-6 (NASB)

Again, when we trust the Lord and don't lean on our own understanding in the healing of memories, we acknowledge Jesus; He takes our *crooked* paths and makes them *straight*. This releases us more *fully* into our destiny because our path to that destiny is now clear and straight with these obstacles removed.

"We look for light, but all is darkness; for brightness, but we walk in deep shadows. Like the blind, we grope along the wall, feeling our way like men without eyes."
Isaiah 59:9b-10a (NIV)

This is another great verse depicting the need for the healing of memories. We really don't want to respond the way we do as we know the right thing (light) to do, but are triggered with the wrong response (darkness). We can't figure out why we are still responding the way we do (deep shadows) as we know what the Word of God says. So we have become blind, groping along the wall, and trying to feel our way without really seeing what the root of our problem is. For it is hidden within our subconscious until the light (Holy Spirit) comes to reveal the memory where our unhealthy responses began.

Isaiah 59:13 says, we have turned away from God, *uttering lies our heart has conceived.* Jesus wants to replace those lies to set us free from what we have believed in childhood; lies that have been keeping us in an emotional prison.

Hosea 10:13 tells us we have eaten the fruit of *lies* and Jesus wants to deliver us from those *lies* and replace them with His truth.

> *"But when He, the Spirit of truth (Holy Spirit) comes,*
> *He will guide you into all truth."*
> John 16:13a (NLT)

I can't emphasize enough how the Holy Spirit does it all and wants to remove *all* our lies and replace them with His truth that makes us free. This is the entire basis of inner healing!

Also, Jesus told us in John 14:12 that whoever believes in Him will do the works He did, and *even GREATER things than these,* because He was going to the Father. When He went to the Father, He sent us the Holy Spirit, Who would be our Teacher, Comforter, and Guide. If the Holy Spirit is in us and is our Guide, He will guide us internally so that our external world is affected as well. The *greater works* are because He sent the Holy Spirit; Jesus knew that the Holy Spirit *in* us was even better than Jesus *with* us.

Then in John 21:25, John also tells us that Jesus did many *OTHER things* than what were recorded in the Bible and if they were all recorded, the whole world wouldn't have room for the books that would contain what He actually did. We probably won't know what those *other* things were until we get to heaven.

If *we see* things done, *other* than what is expressly and clearly written in the Bible, how will we know if they are from God or not? Could it be possible they might be the *greater,* or *other,* works spoken of in the Word? What we need to do is *look at the fruit* to see if what is being produced is good or bad, and remember that a bad tree can't produce good fruit. This *'fruit inspection' is a spiritual law that always operates and never changes,* just like the law of gravity!

We also want to make certain what we see and hear doesn't actually *contradict* any scripture.

The bottom line is:

If lives are being changed, healing occurs, love is produced, joy and peace are the outcome, relationships are being restored, the fruit of the Spirit is evidenced, and behaviors are transformed, that is <u>always</u> GOOD fruit from a GOOD tree!

Another verse tells us:

"What no eye has seen, what no ear has heard, and what <u>no human mind has conceived</u>, the things God has prepared for those who love Him. These are the things God has revealed to us by His Spirit. The Spirit searches all things, even the deep things of God."
I Corinthians 2:9–10 (NIV)

Remember, there are things we *may see and hear* that our human mind can't conceive, so this will be the foundation that will keep us straight and out of deception in the days ahead. When we see something we don't understand, we must *stop and ask* ourselves these questions: *"What is the fruit that I see evidenced from this? Is it good fruit or bad?"*

*"Search me oh God, and know my heart, test me and know my
anxious thoughts and see if there be any hurtful way in
me, and lead me in the everlasting way."*
Psalm 139:24 (NASB)

**Buried deep within our subconscious minds are
painful memories that now cause anxious
thoughts and hurtful ways.**

It takes the Holy Spirit to search our heart to expose our anxious thoughts and hurtful ways. We need *Him* to lead us out of our wrong ways and into His everlasting way, which is peace and love. A *lot* of time is spent on ministering the healing of memories because the *greatest transformations* in people's lives come from this. The outcome, time and time again, is that whatever people struggle with in the present has its origin somewhere in their past. Jesus comes to heal them and transform their lives from a lifetime of wrong thinking, child–like responses, and destructive ways.

The healing of memories *is* following the negative fruit in a person's life back to the root, or where it all began in childhood. Every place their basic need for love and nurture were not met needs inner healing. Some of these responses that need healing might include negative behaviors, wrong attitudes, fears, anxiety, depression, abuse, tragedies, traumatic events, being born into families that practice the occult, and more.

People walk in self–defeating patterns, irrational thoughts, negative emotions, and dysfunctional responses caused by the unhealed pain in their past. They have no idea why they do what they do but they seek help, as they no longer want to continue to live defeated and are *ready* for change.

Remember that we see life through our wounded, painful filters which can either be real or perceived to be real. In either case, our perceptions cause the same feelings and responses to our present circumstances. We think, feel, and respond in our present situations from that place of suppressed pain. It's like a wound that never heals. All it takes for us to perceive that we're hurt again, in the same way, is for someone in the present to rub up against that wound.

> *"And I will give them one heart (a new heart) and I will put*
> *a new spirit within them; and I will take the stony*
> *(unnaturally hardened) heart out of their flesh, and will*
> *give them a heart of flesh (sensitive and responsive*
> *to the touch of their God)."*
> Ezekiel 11:19 (AMP)

This is exactly what Jesus does in the healing of memories. He takes the stony heart out and replaces it with a new heart of flesh. He puts a new spirit within us when we hear Him speak words that replace all our lies, which heals those hurts in our painful memories.

Remember, since Satan is the father of lies, he speaks with false perceptions to a child's mind. Those lies are received as truth and cause a trigger or button that can be pushed when similarly–perceived pain occurs in adulthood. This particular perception follows them into their adult life until it's exposed. Satan speaks lies to us just like he did to Eve when he caused her to eat from the forbidden tree in Genesis 3. Past experiences become strongholds that presently fortify our wrong beliefs, attitudes, and patterns *we* have set up to protect ourselves from perceived pain.

Again, what is happening in the healing of memories? Jesus is accessing our painful memories and showing His Presence in them by using our imagination, which leads to our healing. With this comes revelation and truth that sets people free!

Lord, Your truth revealed in this chapter is resonating with those who need inner healing of memories. They now understand they have wrong responses, attitudes, and behaviors that have roots in their childhood. I declare they will come into such freedom through the work of the Holy Spirit and be transformed from glory to increased glory in their lives. They will be able to respond in love, in those areas where they could only respond in hurtful ways.

In Jesus' name, Amen.

Chapter 9

TRANSFORMED LIVES

We are going to walk through some actual healing of memories so we can understand *how* Jesus heals the pain from our past.

Socially Paralyzed

I want to begin with a personal struggle that Jesus recently healed in the last few years. I have been through so much inner healing during my lifetime and I continue to go through more as the Lord reveals *new* things that are holding me back from walking in my own destiny. It is truly a process in my life!

We are like an onion, where more and more layers are revealed and peeled off as we mature in our walk with the Lord. He doesn't heal everything all at once, and we are in a constant maturing process as the Spirit reveals another layer that needs to be healed. He orchestrates situations in order to expose the next layer, so we are able to see these things and become open to receiving transformation.

We may find ourselves in the middle of situations which cause us to struggle over and over again, without being able to understand why.

We may see the negative fruit it is producing in our lives, but not comprehend or discern the reason behind it. My testimony is one of these cases and an example of the process of healing of memories.

All of my life, I hated being in groups of people. I was more comfortable talking one–on–one, but was irrationally uncomfortable whenever I was in a social situation of more than one person. My sisters had the ability to be warm and friendly in groups, but I couldn't, so I concluded I just wasn't as friendly as they were. I rationalized, buried the pain, and was so *clueless* about the reason for my behavior.

While attending a women's group in our church one night, I saw so clearly there were walls up between myself and the rest of the group. In fighting the usual overwhelming feeling of wanting to leave, I recognized that even though I had walked with the Lord over 40 years, there was this *place* that was still stuck in this old behavior. That night, I decided if I wanted to walk in the destiny the Lord had shown me, I needed to change.

I also had a generational bondage of rejection in my family bloodline and it became a serious struggle over many years. Satan fueled that rejection through circumstances to create lies such as "*No one likes me*," that would keep me in the prison of rejection. Even though I had broken the generational bondage of rejection from my family line years ago, I still had to be healed from the effects of that bondage in my own life.

The majority of inner vows and word curses are revealed during the healing of memories.

As I relate my own experience, you will better understand the process of the healing of memories.

The first thing I did was to give permission to Jesus to go back into my memories to bring me back to the place where this all began in my life; back to the root of why I became paralyzed in group settings.

I was instructed not to try to think of a memory, but invited Jesus to bring the memory to my mind; that memory of where this all began.

This is called, "following the fruit to the root." If we need to pull out a weed (negative fruit), we must get down to the root and make sure it is removed and destroyed, or the weed will grow again. Once the roots are fully pulled up, that weed will not be able to grow back.

The Holy Spirit brought me to a memory of a situation that happened when I was in 5th grade. Every day I walked home from school and there was a group of older boys who walked the same route. They would bully and taunt me, saying very hurtful things. When I got home, my grandfather would call me a whore because of all the boys around me. During the healing of memories ministry time, I asked Jesus to show me how I felt. I didn't understand it at the time, but because I was still believing all the lies the boys spoke, there were many feelings Jesus brought to the surface, such as embarrassment, anger, rejection, hurt, fear, and more. He also showed me I had feelings of shame when my grandfather called me a whore and how I had come to believe the entire situation was all my fault.

As an adult, the trigger from this memory caused me to put up walls of self–protection. Social situations made me uncomfortable and caused me to want to leave. All of this happened in my subconscious mind and I *never understood* the reason why, after walking with the Lord all of these years, I was still feeling like this. For example, I would always leave for home after Sunday services instead of staying to talk with people. I didn't want to be like that but didn't know then, what I know now about the healing of memories. I was certainly surprised to find all of this was still buried in my subconscious mind, thinking this entire time that *I was just being me.* I was so wrong!

When Jesus shows us how we felt in the memory, we know these are the places where lies were believed and need to be replaced with His truth. By Jesus taking me into this memory, He revealed how I felt when the incident was occurring.

I asked Jesus to come into that memory. He never leaves us or forsakes us, so it was easy for me to imagine, sense, or see Him being in that scenario with me. He began to speak to me and told me how much He loved me and had protected me, even though I didn't know Him during that time. He told me none of the things the boys said were true and none of it was my fault, but also revealed I had been believing what they said about me. Jesus showed me I had made an inner vow, *"No one likes me,"* so we broke the power of that covenant with Satan's lie in prayer. That's one of the reasons why I couldn't function in groups and didn't have any close friends while growing up, because I believed the lie that *"No one likes me."* The power of that lie caused me to become a prisoner, even after 40 years of walking with God. The inner vow was buried and long forgotten, but still operating in my life until I received inner healing.

Jesus also showed me how my Italian grandfather was un-schooled and ignorant, and projected onto me what he was taught as a young boy growing up in Italy. The Lord assured me that what my grandfather spoke was not the truth, or how Jesus saw me. Jesus replaced every lie I was believing from childhood, with His truth and made me free.

Remember this verse?

"You shall know the truth and the truth shall make you free."
John 8:32 (NASB)

With Jesus' words to me, I was filled with compassion for my grandfather and forgave him and the boys for what they had done. Jesus transformed that entire memory from painful to being healed, from being in bondage because of the lies I didn't even remember I believed, to the truth that made me free.

Even though I had no memory of this incident in the present, when Jesus accessed that memory, I remembered, and it all came flooding back to me. I had *no clue* that this incident was the cause of my present paralyzing feelings in social situations.

While in high school, I lived close enough to walk to school every day. As an adult, I was able to remember being unable to walk past groups of kids congregated in front of the school. I would cross the street to go around them and then cross again to get into the school door. I can easily recall that I could not look at any of the kids while walking down the hallways; I kept my eyes glued to the floor. But these *weren't* the memories of where it all began. Jesus knew the starting point of the pain, so when I invited Him to reveal the root cause, the Holy Spirit brought me back to that event in 5th grade. High School events and adulthood situations were only triggers for my *suppressed* and irrational feelings and responses.

I didn't have an opportunity, for several months, to test the results of my healing. Then I was invited to another women's group and went, anxious to see the fruit of my encounter with the Lord. My post–healing experience was as different as day and night. Instead of acting withdrawn, I was a social butterfly. I was able to be warm, friendly, open, talkative, and all the things I could never do during the years I was trapped in that emotional prison. The situations that used to push that trigger or button *had* the power to cause me pain. But no more! I can't really express how much the healing of this memory has totally and radically changed my life. I am *so* thankful to the Lord!

This is exactly how it works for each person who is struggling with painful wounds. There is *always* a root cause of the fruit we actually see in our life.

A woman who attends my church told me she saw such a difference in how I was able to reach out in openness and a *freedom* she hadn't seen there before. Instead of people avoiding me because of the walls of self–protection I projected, they were now drawn in. Praise be to His name!

When we are emotionally healed, we are launched further into destiny.

I was so totally and radically changed in that healing of memories and feel it has launched me further into my destiny. I can now be open, friendly, and talk to others no matter where we are or who is there. Social events are no longer a problem!

My response and behavior was instantly changed when Jesus came into my memory and replaced all those lies, I didn't even know I was believing, with His truths and freedom. That which was hidden in darkness was brought into His light, and the enemy lost his stronghold in my life to keep me in prison and unable to walk in what was written on my scroll of destiny.

Imagine someone who has 'ministering to the masses' written in their book in heaven but is paralyzed in social situations. That person would not be able to connect and bond with the groups of people whom the Lord is calling them to, which would greatly hinder their ability to minister. With all the walls of social fear erected between the minister and the people, it would also *severely* limit the people's ability to receive ministry.

We can certainly understand how the enemy would want to foster this fear in a person's life to prevent them from walking in their destiny. Satan knows that we would damage his kingdom of darkness and become a force to be reckoned with if we are freed from his bondages and lies. The good news is that God loves us, wants us free, whole, able to fulfill our heart's desires, and live out what is written in our book.

It is such a blessing and so awesome to be able to see the results with those who receive inner healing. There are so many testimonies of lives that have been radically changed by Jesus coming in to heal the memories where pain and lies began. The memories are still there, but the hurt feelings associated with them are all removed and healed. The *best* news is that our current responses are now *permanently* changed.

I want to share some more examples of healing of memories so we can see the types of bondages and transformations needed in people's lives, and how Jesus healed them.

This next one is a written testimony from a woman attending an inner healing conference.

Control Issues

"At a recent conference, in the healing of memories portion of the teachings, I was asked if I would be willing to have one of my issues healed in front of the audience. When asked what my biggest struggle was, I replied that I had issues with control and that is where we started.

"In addressing this fruit of control in my life, I asked Jesus to show me where this issue began. He took me back to a memory of an event which occurred when I was 6 or 7 years old. In the memory, I was leaning over the balustrade of the second floor of my childhood home, pleading with my father not to hurt my mom. He was very drunk and angry. I was terrified he would hurt her because he had grabbed her arm and was shaking her.

"I asked Jesus to show me how I felt at that time. There were so many strong feelings that surfaced – great fear, dread, anxiety, anger directed toward my father, feelings of responsibility, anger at my mom that I was put in this role of protecting her, and anger that she didn't do something to stop my dad. The biggest revelation that came was I felt that if I took control of the situation and stopped my dad, then nothing bad would happen. This was a lie that followed me into my adult life, where *I felt I had to control situations so nothing bad would happen.* This inner vow needed to be broken!

"Next I asked Jesus to come into the memory . . . He pulled me into His arms and said; 'This is not your responsibility because your mom and dad were in the middle of their own struggles and pain, and that's all they were capable of doing.'

"I received the Holy Spirit's comfort in the midst of that traumatic situation, His love for my mom and dad and how I needed to forgive them. In prayer, I told both my mom and my dad that I forgave them and no longer held them accountable for what they did. I wept at the overwhelming release and healing this brought, and my husband came up from the audience to comfort me. I realized my need to control situations and people around me came from my fear that *bad things would happen if I didn't take control*. My control issues had affected my relationships with people, especially my husband.

"It had always been my habit to jump into situations uninvited and take over, which caused a lot of conflicts. Since the healing session, I have experienced great deliverance from the need to control. Jesus ministered His perspective and replaced my lies with His truth. I have been freed from that anger and hurt, and no longer have the fear and dread of something bad happening. I am also able to trust God more, am relaxed, and enjoying my relationships. My husband is *very* grateful for this change in me, and so am I."

All this was hidden in this woman's life, where she never saw or understood why she needed to control people and situations, until this miraculous healing took place. Isn't the Lord so good?

Imagine we are destined to walk in a leadership position but have control issues in our life.

This would greatly affect our ability to lead others and cause great *conflicts*, as people wouldn't like being controlled. This would really hinder the relationships we have, and may cause others to leave because they can't tolerate our control. It would certainly impede our destiny and our ability to be successful in leading others effectively.

Satan knows just what is necessary to prevent us from walking in our destiny, but the awesome news is that Jesus came to set us free so we fulfill what is written in our book!

Can't Tell Them How I Feel

There was a woman who struggled with telling people how she was really feeling and wanted that changed in her life. She asked Jesus to take her to the memory of where it all began. Suddenly she could see herself as a toddler in the kitchen having breakfast with her father. He was trying to get her to eat soft boiled eggs with crackers and told her she wasn't going to leave without eating them. She replied that she didn't like them, but he forced the spoon and eggs into her mouth. This made her cry and become so upset that she threw up all over him. His response was to angrily clear the dishes and slam things around.

She asked Jesus to show her how she felt in this situation and He revealed she had been scared, felt powerless, and unheard. Because her dad was angry, she also believed she had to do what she was told in order to be loved. The floodgates opened for her on that particular emotion. She felt hurt, rejected, a burden, and that children should be seen and not heard. Jesus showed her some inner vows she made at that time. Remember, inner vows are lies that keep us in bondage. These lies Jesus revealed were: *"I will not tell people how I feel because I won't be accepted."* The other was, *"I'm not good enough for people to want me around."*

Inner healing was necessary for this woman because childhood trauma caused her to feel that she wasn't allowed to speak up for herself. We broke the inner vows she had made which prevented her, as an adult, from being able to express her true feelings.

The feelings Jesus shows a person are a key to the lies they have been believing. When someone comes for ministry, notes are taken and we write down what feelings Jesus shows them. Sometimes, some of the feelings are healed when the Lord speaks, but not all of them at once. If a person is not fully healed, we go back to the particular feelings that still need healing prayer and allow Jesus to do more.

Remember the story of the blind man in Mark 8:24, who only saw men as trees when Jesus first prayed, and how He needed to pray for him again to receive his complete healing. We pray until they are fully healed in that memory.

This woman asked Jesus to come into that memory to heal her. In her imagination, she saw His face of compassion toward her and trusted Him to heal her. He said, "*I've got your back,*" then wrapped His arms around her and told her to look at her dad. With Jesus' ministry to her, she felt protected and safe from her dad. Jesus showed her during that childhood incident, she lost her ability to have a voice and He gave it back to her. She forgave her Dad for this incidence and can now tell people how she is feeling. She is no longer bound by the lies from the painful memory that were triggered every time she needed to speak up but couldn't.

After the healing of this memory, this woman can walk free from those childhood lies. She is able to say things to people that she never was able to articulate before, and can graciously make her true feelings known. For the first time in her marriage, she is able to speak up and share her honest opinion with her husband. She feels like a different person; a free person.

Jesus is so good and wants us to walk in complete freedom. All we have to do is appropriate what He already did for us on the cross.

**The enemy is ecstatic when he can prevent us
from being able to fulfill our destiny.**

Imagine this woman's destiny was to be a teacher and she couldn't speak up. How would she be able to walk in her destiny, and how many people who needed what she has to teach would never receive that important information because of her fear? It doesn't have to stay this way as there is freedom available from the Lord because He wants this for us even more than we do!

Not Good Enough

This same woman also felt nothing she ever did was good enough. She asked Jesus to take her back to the memory of where it all began. Jesus led her to remember when her mom brought her stepdad's two daughters to live with them; this happened when she was eight years old. Because she was a compliant child, she did things exactly as her mother instructed, but the other girls would not. Because her mother didn't want to appear to be favoring her own daughter, she decided to treat all three girls the same regardless of whether they obeyed or not. So after cleaning their rooms, her mom would frequently go into all three, empty their closets, toy chests, and all their drawers into the middle of the floor and make them put it all back properly.

The woman asked Jesus to show her how she felt at that time, and He revealed that she felt it wasn't fair and if her stepsisters hadn't been there, she wouldn't have been treated as though she was disobedient. She resented the girls and also felt angry that her mom, as an adult, always had to have things done her way. Some inner vows were revealed in this memory.

"Nothing is good enough and nothing I ever do is right." The enemy spoke this lie to her and she came into agreement with it as a child, because of her pain. In the present, she was stuck in an emotional prison because of this lie.

It seemed to her that her mom always pointed out things which were wrong and never pointed out things she did right. The other vow was really a bitter root judgment against her mother. *"She always has to have things done her way or the highway."* This affected her relationship with her mother and became the filter she heard through after that.

We broke both of these vows and then she asked Jesus to come into that memory. Jesus assured her that He was with her and reached out to draw her to sit on His lap. He hugged her and she was filled with peace.

Everyone has unique needs during the healing ministry, so we simply follow the leading of the Holy Spirit until freedom and transformation come and all the pain from those feelings is gone.

This woman forgave her mother and stepsisters. Her life became whole and free from the feeling that nothing she did was good enough. She testifies to the change that came after Jesus healed her memory of this incident in her youth. She is able to do things without all those negative lies, interwoven in everything she did.

She recently returned from a mission trip and stated that both healings she received made such a huge difference in her ability to minister to others. Life has changed for the better!

Before receiving healing of memories, many of us may see God through the filter of *nothing I do is good enough.* Even though the Bible teaches us the truth, and we can quote it, the lies of the enemy continue to hold us back from our destiny until they are uncovered and healed.

As an adult, if we believe the lies that *nothing is good enough* and *we never do anything right*, that belief becomes a great obstacle to *anything* written on our scroll of destiny. It will prevent us from being able to step out to fulfill that which God has purposed. It doesn't matter what we are called to do if we are held in an emotional prison. If we believe nothing we do is good enough, we will *never* step out to accomplish the great things written in our book. We remain locked in the spiritual law that says, "*as a man thinks in his heart, so is he.*"

Children fill in the gaps with their own reality, which become lies that keep them bound as adults.

Let's try to understand how unhealed pain operates in our adult life. If someone says something we hear through our fil-ter "*I'm not good enough*", it pushes a button from childhood and we respond in ways that are not Christlike. We may re-spond from hurt and anger, but when the root is healed, then we will be able to hear the *very same thing* from that person without feeling pain or reacting with a wrong response.

When Jesus heals the memory of where it all began, He also heals the pain of all subsequent hurts in that area. Remember, the memory of where the pain began is the root cause; it is beneath the surface and unseen. All the pain and ungodly re-sponses which occur after the initial hurt are like the weed which grows in the open. We need to get the root out so the weed dies and doesn't grow again.

When the initial pain is healed, the pain from that point on is also healed. We don't need to go through and heal every time we feel that same type of hurt after the original wounding. The pain is healed and gone from that point forward. The trigger or button which causes more pain and wrong responses is now gone and no longer operates in our present circumstances.

This inner healing of the soul is *crucial* in a person's life. We can receive a tremendous physical healing from a disease, yet *still* be in an emotional prison. The healing of a soul is *just as miraculous* and transforming as a physical healing. We need healing in both our body *and* soul to become totally whole!

People may stand in long lines or go to a service for prayer to receive a physical healing they need. My prayer is that we will begin to see people lining up to receive a *healing for their soul*. I also pray for people to begin to see the *miraculous* found in a transformed life; for it truly is a sign and a wonder!

Lord, I declare those reading these testimonies will begin to see the negative 'fruit' in their lives that needs healing of memories. I declare roots revealed, all lies exposed, and Jesus to heal those areas of their life, so they can walk in freedom and wholeness. Lord, that through this healing, they will be more fully released into their destiny!

In Jesus' name, Amen.

ALL THE DAYS ORDAINED FOR ME
WERE WRITTEN IN YOUR BOOK BEFORE
ONE OF THEM CAME TO BE.
PSALM 139:16 (NIV)

Chapter 10

PRINCIPLES AND DESTINY

I want to share some principles to follow in the healing of memories ministry for ourselves and others.

Within these principles, there is great freedom of the Holy Spirit to move, lead, and speak into the situations He reveals in order to heal us and set us free.

It's extremely important for the person with the memory not to *rationalize* in their childhood situation. A child is *incapable* of rationalizing the way adults are able to, and this will hinder the healing of their memory.

When they start rationalizing, we redirect them to being back in the childhood memory and how they were *actually* feeling as a child. Otherwise, it will be difficult to get to those childhood lies that have them bound as adults.

PRINCIPLES FOR HEALING
OF MEMORIES

Always begin and end each inner healing session with prayer. Before you begin, invite the Holy Spirit to lead both you and the person being ministered to. Also pray that there will be no negative *spiritual backlash*, as a result of any ministry taking place during the session; covering all persons involved, as well as homes and families.

After you have finished the session, pray for the Spirit to *seal* the healing He ministered in the person's life.

Below are principles for the healing of memories sessions

1. **The person identifies the struggle they have in their present life.** The place to start would be the reason why they came in for healing: the trigger in their present life. When you identify the negative fruit, ask them this question, "When this happens, how does that make you feel?" This will reveal the actual root that needs healing, such as fear, feeling unloved, rejected, guilt, shame, unsafe, angry, etc.

2. *They* **invite Jesus to bring them to the memory of where this all began.** Instruct the person not to try to think of a memory, but to allow the Holy Spirit to bring the memory into their mind; into their imagination. *He* is faithful to bring them back to the *root* memory which causes their negative current response.

3. **Once they have the memory, *they* ask Jesus to show them how it made them feel.** Sometimes the Lord may speak into *your* spirit, but rather than tell the person what you are hearing, pose it as a question so *Jesus tells them the answer.* You may hear "*unloved,*" and instruct them to ask Jesus if they felt unloved. They are *changed* when they hear *Him* speak to them directly and not when *you* tell them what He said. You should also write down all the feelings He shows them.

4. **They invite Jesus to come into that memory to bring healing.** Jesus *always* does or says something to bring healing and freedom from the pain and lies that memory has produced. Before ending the session, ask them from their list, if they still feel the ways He revealed to them. If some of those emotions are still unhealed, have them ask Jesus to speak into that feeling. An example would be, "*Jesus was this my fault?*" When He answers them, they are set free. It may be that all their lives, people may have told them it wasn't their fault, but they have never been able to come out of this *underlying* belief until they hear Jesus speak *His* truth to them.

5. **Lead them in a prayer of forgiveness for those who hurt them.** Depending upon the situation, forgiveness is extended to people who hurt them, but they may also need to forgive themselves or God.

It's so amazing what the Lord does to bring transformation to a wounded heart, which results in a deeper release into destiny. Isn't Jesus good? He loves us so much that He comes to open our prison door and remove our chains. Then we are able to live the abundant life He came to give us, and walk more fully in our destiny.

FINDING OUR DESTINY

Now we can understand why so many of us are not walking in the destiny written in our book in heaven. I hope our explorations into the power of inner healing have clarified how lies from our childhood can relegate us to a life of mediocrity and prevent us from walking in the fullness of our destiny. Triggers which cause wrong responses, prevent us from walking in love and being conformed to the image of Christ. Such bad fruit is reaped from those lies, unforgiveness, word curses, inner vows, and ungodly soul ties.

Inner healing exposes the lies and replaces them with the truth of who Jesus says we are. With these lies removed, we can finally understand our identity and how much God truly loves us. Living in that newly realized truth propels us further into the destiny in which God intended us to walk all along.

Let us always remember this wonderful verse regarding the destiny that was written in our book before we were born.

"Your eyes saw my unformed body; all the days ordained for me were written in your book before one of them came to be."
Psalm 139:16 (NIV)

It's time to go through inner healing to remove the obstacles from our lives, so we can live out *everything* that is written in our book.

We *also* need to see and understand what our destiny is and what is actually written on our pages. God told Jeremiah that while he was in the womb, he was called, appointed, and anointed to be a prophet. So where do we begin to understand what *is written in our personal scrolls?*

Our destiny is understood through our spirit man which was made alive when we became born again. The Holy Spirit *wants* to reveal our destiny to us!

We can *begin* by looking at our interests, strengths, passions, and deep desires. The activities and pursuits which excite, compel, satisfy, and fulfill us are key indications of the gifting, calling, strengths, abilities, appointments, and anointing which define our destiny. You may wish to create a list of those major interests, strengths, passions, and desires; as they can reveal some of the foundational qualities of *your* design and lead you to understand where you are heading and what is written in your book. Feel free to ask significant authority figures, who know you well, to add their insights to this list.

The story of Joseph, found in Genesis 37–41, reveals a common thread of destiny that was traceable throughout a lifetime of difficult circumstances. Joseph was born to govern, to be in charge and manage people, but he had much to learn before he was ready for God's ultimate plan. While still a teenager living at home, he tried to manage his brothers, but they were offended at his efforts and decided to teach him a lesson by selling him into slavery. After a time, he was sold to Potiphar, chief executioner of Pharaoh's royal guard in Egypt, and eventually became supervisor of his house. When further complications led to an accusation of rape, Joseph was thrown in prison. Very shortly, his gifting put him in a position to be in charge of all the prisoners. Because of his faithfulness and integrity in those trying circumstances, Joseph's reputation came to the attention of the Pharaoh himself, who called the young man out of prison to interpret his disturbing dream. In God's time, Joseph was elevated to the position of supervising the entire nation. We can stand back and see that throughout his life, Joseph walked in leadership roles in *every* situation he found himself in; each trial was actually a step further in fulfilling his ultimate destiny. It would be safe to say that governing was written in his book.

We may not be called to govern but, if we could get a bird's eye view of our own life, we would be able to see the pattern or thread of passion, positioning, gifting, and tendencies that reveal our calling and destiny.

I tend to believe that before governing the nation of Egypt, Joseph didn't realize how he was actually walking in leadership in every place he was sent. He was simply doing what came naturally, without being aware that his dreams were coming true. Even though he didn't comprehend the steps, God was still preparing him to fulfill his destiny and walk in the fullness of his calling. Obstacles in his life needed to be overcome and deep character developed before he fulfilled his ultimate destiny.

When he was a teenager in his father's house, Joseph had no idea that his dreams meant he would one day save an entire nation from starvation. Dreams are not literal, but speak figuratively to us and need interpretation to be understood. As a young man, Joseph dreamed his brothers' wheat sheaves bowed down to his. He didn't have the correct interpretation at that time but so many years later, the dream was fulfilled when his brothers came to Egypt for wheat and submissively bowed before Joseph, the great governor of Egypt.

Each life test Joseph passed was used to prepare him to accomplish what was written in his scroll; we are each prepared in the same way. Like Joseph, we may have had dreams we don't yet understand. Perhaps prophetic words have been spoken over our lives that we have not yet seen fulfilled. We may have been given a vision that gives us a clue about our destiny and purpose, but like Joseph, we don't fully comprehend how it will come to pass. If you have been given any dreams, visions, or prophetic words, write them down. They will be a great indication to understanding your destiny.

The truth is, God has a destiny for each one of us. My heart is to see everyone set so completely free that we will be able to walk in those assignments, positions, careers, creativity, and so much more. My deep desire is to see lives released into their destinies and I believe inner healing is being used for this purpose.

I encourage you to pursue inner healing and turn from anything that presents an obstacle to birthing what you carry. The time has come for you to walk in the magnificent destiny the Lord has written in your scroll. Your destiny may not appear to have the magnitude of Joseph's, but it will bring you great delight, fulfillment, and will accomplish for others what God intends. The Lord gives each of us the desires of our heart, which means that He gifts us with the desires that will fulfill the destiny He planned before we were formed in our mother's womb. You carry a God–designed purpose and destiny, and according to Psalm 37:4, He delights in helping you fulfill it.

We are not all called to the same destinies, but each destiny is uniquely tailored by the Lord. *He knows your personality, desires, needs, thought processes, and skills.* Your calling is customized for you alone and will reflect the Lord's intentions for you and all those who receive what you have to give in the way you give it. God's plan *suits* our individual personality, wants, needs, and how we think, as He *knows* how we are created. Some of us are more creative, while others are more structured in their thinking. All of this will determine what we will be called to do. If we are destined to be in government, then we will need a more structured way of thinking and doing things. If we are called to be an artist, then we can't be as structured and need to be creative in our thinking.

God knows us so intimately and chooses just the right destiny for us.

Happiness, love, peace, joy, fulfillment, and great contentment are found in living out our destiny. I am not saying life won't throw us curves and we won't be in difficult situations, but we will also find great contentment in fulfilling what we were destined to do. The freer we become, the more we will comprehend, and walk in the awesome, spectacular destiny the Lord planned for each of us before we were born.

Let the Lord have His way in our life and allow Him to heal our body, soul, and spirit.

"May God Himself, the God of peace, sanctify you through and through. May your whole spirit, soul and body be kept blameless at the coming of our Lord Jesus Christ."
I Thessalonians 5:23 (NIV)

One meaning of sanctify is *'to be set apart, consecrated, and made holy.'* Another definition is *'to be free from sin, purified, cleansed, unburdened, and redeemed.'* This second meaning is very applicable to the process of inner healing. We each need to have our spirit, soul, and body sanctified; free from sin, purified, cleansed, unburdened, and redeemed until Jesus comes again. Paul prayed this for the Thessalonians and I come into agreement with this for you.

May you fulfill the wonderful destiny that has been written in your book in heaven, with *all* hindrances and obstacles removed from your path. Seek inner healing from everything in your life that is keeping you from peace, happiness, and contentment with others, yourself, and in your relationship with God.

Lord, I declare that everyone reading this book will now see and understand the great importance of inner healing. Holy Spirit, place the desire in hearts to have every obstacle removed from their life so they will be able to fulfill the great destiny You have for them.

Lord, release them into all You have written in their book and show them what is written on the scroll of destiny You have put within them, to be fulfilled in their lifetime.

I declare they are in a new season and these world changers will hear the new sound in heaven being released upon the earth to raise up the mighty army of God that will so impact this world and bring in the greatest harvest we have ever seen!

In the name of Jesus, Amen...

Remember you *are* "Designed for Destiny"!

ALL THE DAYS ORDAINED FOR ME
WERE WRITTEN IN YOUR BOOK BEFORE
ONE OF THEM CAME TO BE.
PSALM 139:16 (NIV)

Chapter 11

A CALL TO HELP

While waiting for more of my own destiny to be revealed, the Lord called me to start Reformation Center and showed me the *first* ministry that needed to be established in our center was inner healing. We named it *Transformation Healing* and God showed me the reason it was to be the first, was that it is the foundational ministry for the other ministries which would be established later.

Before beginning this inner healing ministry, I was given a prophetic word that *Transformation Healing* would be a ministry for the downtrodden. I looked up the definition of downtrodden to gain a better understanding of what this ministry would accomplish. It means *'to be oppressed or treated badly by people in power.'* Some synonyms are: *'oppressed, subjugated, persecuted, repressed, tyrannized, crushed, enslaved, exploited, victimized, bullied, powerless, helpless, abused, and maltreated.'* This really sounded to me like a whole lot of people who needed inner healing!

The Lord also gave me this verse:

"When He saw the crowds, He was moved with compassion for them, because they were <u>harassed</u> <u>and</u> <u>helpless</u>, like sheep with-out a shepherd. Then He said to His disciples, "<u>The</u> <u>harvest</u> <u>is</u> <u>plentiful</u>, <u>but</u> <u>the</u> <u>workers</u> <u>are</u> <u>few</u>."
Matthew 9:36–37 (BSB)

To understand who Jesus was referring to in this verse, we need to understand what harassed means. The definition is, *'stressed out, worried, worn out, hard pressed, tormented with troubles and cares, bothered continually, persecuted, and trou-bled by repeated attacks.'* Again, these are people who sound like they really need inner healing in their lives.

The good news is, Jesus was moved with compassion on us and is also raising up those who have *His* same heart of com-passion to minister inner healing to those who are harassed and helpless. People have destiny written over their lives into which Jesus wants them fully released.

We can either be part of the problem or part of the solution. The solution is to have the same kind of compassion as Jesus and become one who sets these captives free by opening their prison doors. Jesus tells us to ask the Lord to send out workers into the harvest field to minister to those harassed and help-less people. Reformation Center has answered that call and yet there are *so many* more workers needed as the field is ripe and ready, but the workers are few. Will we hear the call and re-ceive His compassion for those who are harassed with no one to help them?

I want to share some things we need to understand, concern-ing the inner healing ministry.

Again, many physical illnesses with their root in past childhood hurts and traumas may be relieved through inner healing. We have seen numerous healings take place during ministry times, including vocal chords no longer needing surgery, back pain being relieved, gallbladder pain alleviated, and depression lifted. These miracles took place without praying specifically for the illnesses, but came from the person's inner healing sessions after they were made emotionally whole. I am just amazed at how the Lord does this over and over again!

At one of our conferences, there was a teaching on forgiveness and then we led people in corporate prayer. We saw a healing from migraine headaches that was such a painful problem in this woman's life. Another person had bone spurs on their feet which are terribly painful and make walking nearly impossible, but the Lord healed them. We didn't specifically pray for these physical healings, but the root behind them was unforgiveness. Their testimony was, when we led them in prayer *to forgive* others, themselves, and God, they were instantly healed.

All illnesses are not healed during inner healing, but many which are rooted in unforgiveness, bitterness, and stress may be healed.

There are also some things the Lord spoke and revealed to me in preparation to minister inner healing to people. I want to share some of them with you to assist you in helping others receive inner healing.

The Lord spoke something to me that changed my understanding and became a revelation of *how* to minister the healing of memories. He asked me if I remembered receiving a specific revelation. I recalled several revelations and the fact that I

113

tried to share them with others who didn't seem to grasp them at that time. Six months later those same people came to me so excited about what God revealed to them, and it turned out to be exactly what I had tried to share with them earlier. The Lord also reminded me of the times that others shared things with me that I wasn't able to receive until sometime later. I remembered both those examples, but never understood the reason for them. It was puzzling to me how that happened. What came next cleared up everything and *transformed* my understanding when the Lord said:

"People don't change when *you* tell them what I am saying; they only change when *I* tell them what I am saying."

Wow! This was a *great revelation* to me and I knew I had to make a change, as I hear God speak to me when I minister to others. I was *not* to tell people what I saw and heard, but to ask them questions so they were able to hear God's voice for themselves. He made it quite *clear*, people wouldn't be healed by what I told them He was saying, but would be transformed by hearing *Him* speak to them directly; just like in the examples He gave me.

Since this understanding, I have shifted to serving as a facilitator between the person and Jesus. As a facilitator, my job is to *ask questions* and let the person hear the answers from Jesus. As a result, I witness radical transformations and release from emotional prisons. This has transformed how I minister! God loves us all so much that He wants us to hear Him for ourselves so we are healed from everything that keeps us from fully living out what is written in our book in heaven. As an example, if I hear the Holy Spirit say, *"bitterness,"* I tell them to ask Jesus if they have been feeling bitter. It has become so much easier to minister to others as I just ask the questions the Holy Spirit gives me and He does *all* the healing. It is so amazing!

There is something else I heard from God's heart about how He feels about those trapped in sin. There was a certain man who went to another ministry looking to be healed from depression. He was told he was walking in sin and first needed to repent and turn away from that sin before he could receive ministry. He called me and related what had happened and asked if I felt the same way. I inquired of the Lord, as to what He had to say in reference to what happened to this man.

The week prior, we had gone out to pray for people on the streets. Beforehand, the Holy Spirit had shown me earbuds, so I looked for someone listening to music. I saw a Hispanic boy and an adult woman sitting on a bench; the boy had earbuds on, listening to music. I approached them and found the woman spoke no English, so the boy translated between us. She said she had severe back pain and was going to the doctor to schedule surgery for her agonizing pain. I prayed for her, she was completely healed, and was totally *amazed* at what God had done.

So, in asking the Lord how he felt about the man who called me, the Lord asked *me* a series of questions. "That woman who was healed, was she a drug addict? Was she committing adultery? Was she abusing her children? Was she a prostitute?" I had to keep answering each of those questions with, "I don't know." Then He told me something that cleared this all up for me:

"Get them healed and they will be able to make better decisions."

He told me that if He healed *her* He would also heal the man, and when the man was healed, he would be able to make better decisions.

Jesus always healed and never qualified people as to whether they were in sin. After they were healed is when He told them in John 5:14, to go and sin no more. Jesus healed every disease and sickness according to Mathew 9:35–36, as He was moved with compassion on people who were suffering. This revelation really impacted how I saw people from that moment forth.

Many years ago, I also had a dream I didn't understand and hadn't seen come to pass. In the dream, I was with my husband and others in a restaurant sitting around a large table. I got up, walked to the back of the room to some large windows, and looked out to see below me a forest with a clearing full of wild and domestic animals. Every one of them was pregnant with no one to help with the birth and I knew I was to go down to assist them.

The first animal I approached was groaning in pain, as she couldn't give birth because the baby was breech. I put my hands and arms into the womb and had to turn the baby 180 degrees so the head was in the proper position in the birth canal. The moment the head was in the correct place, the mother immediately gave birth. I went to the next animal and found her in the same situation. I once again moved the baby into position and it was immediately born.

That was the case in 100 percent of the animals in the dream. Each time I put my hands into the womb and turned a baby, it was *immediately* born. I woke up wondering what this meant; I knew in my spirit it was a dream from God. Someone gave me the interpretation which resonated with me. She told me she heard God saying to her spirit that this dream was about birthing destinies. People's destinies were breech and couldn't be birthed without someone to assist them and for years, that's all I understood. This reminds me of Joseph and his dream about his brothers bowing to him, as we both didn't understand our dreams.

When Reformation Center started and I realized inner healing would be the first ministry in the center, the Lord asked me if I remembered that dream. He said to me, "This is that!" At that, I finally understood this inner healing ministry is the interpretation and fulfillment of the dream about turning the breech babies into the right position.

Inner healing will bring people into the right position for their destiny to be birthed.

Our destiny (baby) is hindered until our obstacles (breech position) are removed. As with the animals in my dream, as soon as the head (inner healing) is in the proper position, the birth of our destiny is quickly accomplished. What an awesome picture of people walking in freedom and wholeness.

There are so many reasons why we don't walk in the fullness of our destiny, and my heart is to help people see many of these obstacles and hindrances which are keeping them back from being everything they are meant to be. The *great* news is, there is a remedy for removing them from your life! Seek inner healing for all those obstacles and hindrances, standing in the way of your destiny!

My heart in writing this book is for *you* to receive inner healing, freedom, and wholeness; then be able to use this book to help *others* obtain their freedom and wholeness. You will find all the individual topics we covered, as well as the inner healing prayers, listed in the table of contents for your easy reference.

Lord, I pray everyone reading this book will see how much You love them and that You have a plan for their life. I declare they will realize You desire to see them walking free, whole, and able to fulfill the great destiny You have written in their book in heaven. I also pray that they will live life excited and with purpose! As they seek You through the ministry of inner healing, may all their lies, triggers of pain, obstacles, and hindrances be replaced by Your truth. I declare freedom and wholeness, and that their souls and lives will prosper.

In Jesus' name, Amen!

You are truly *Designed for Destiny*!

Note: Please continue reading to discover our *Guide* available as a workbook, to be used as a learning companion to *Designed for Destiny.* There is also information regarding our first book *Secrets Revealed,* and a prayer on the last page.

Designed for Destiny - Guide

We designed a *Guide,* to be used as a workbook for *Designed for Destiny,* and created to enhance and reinforce what we are learning about inner healing. It is meant to be used as a tool to equip people for ministry, individually or in small groups.

Did you know science has found, when people *read and write* what they are learning, it *greatly* increases their learning and retention rate? This book is designed to help us *learn and retain more,* by answering questions which focus on key points relevant to the healing process.

Many questions in this book are personalized for the reader and include personalized prayers, as well as questions to help each person begin to understand their destiny and what they were created to do.

There is a complete list of generational sins, illnesses, and the occult provided in the *Guide* to assist in identifying generational bondages in our family line.

If you would like to lead a small group using this *Guide,* there is a free *Leader's Guide* available on the website below.

You can order *Designed for Destiny – Guide* on our website at: www.ReformationCenter.net/designed-for-destiny.

You may also order it on Amazon.

Secrets Revealed

A Journey Into Kingdom Principles

In chapter 10 of *Designed for Destiny*, we learned about Joseph, his dream, and his destiny. If you would like to glean so much more from Joseph's journey to fulfill what God had written in his scroll, please read *Secrets Revealed – A Journey into Kingdom Principles*. You may order the book on our website at: www.ReformationCenter.net/secrets–revealed, and it's also available on Amazon.

Secrets are waiting for you!

Secrets are stored up in the Word of God for those who seek them out, for those who have a heart to know the purposes of God for their lives and for the earth.

Secrets Revealed shares many Kingdom Principles that will release destiny in our life. God's principles will transform us as we receive revelation from scripture and have life experiences that thrust us deeper into the Kingdom of God.

Do you want to:

- walk in greater authority here on earth and in the spirit realm?
- learn about spheres of authority?
- understand what honor looks like?

- become a warrior?
- minister with angels?
- understand how to be promoted?
- walk in creative power?
- understand divine order from heaven to earth?
- learn how to walk in an open heaven?
- understand how to move from your dream into destiny?
- learn many other secret Kingdom principles?

If so, this book will get you there! *Secrets Revealed* shares many Kingdom Principles to help transform our life and prepare us to carry the weight of God's glory and authority every day of our life.

"He reveals the deep and secret things..."
Daniel 2:22 (KJB 2000)

Meet the Author

Linda Santangelo is Senior Leader and founder of Reformation Center, whose vision is "Restoring God's Original Design." Her desire is to see individuals and regions walking out the love of the Father in every realm to which they are called and to see them being released into their destiny.

She is an ordained minister, passionate speaker, and apostolic teacher whose life pursuit is to see lives and regions transformed.

Her desire is to see reformation come to individuals, churches, regions and nations, and to see them released into the authority of the Kingdom and supernatural realms.

She has a heart to see the five–fold ministry restored to the Church in order to establish the government of the Kingdom of God from heaven to earth.

Linda lives in Florida with her husband Vinnie, and has four children and two granddaughters.

She has authored these books: *Secrets Revealed – A Journey into Kingdom Principles, Designed for Destiny,* and *Designed for Destiny – Guide.*

Her inner healing training comes from sitting under anointed men and women of God who teach inner healing. Some of those schools/books are: John & Paula Sandford, *The Transformation of the Inner Man* and training CD's; Henry Wright, *A More Excellent Way,* training CD's and healing conferences; Randy Clark, *Ministry Team Training Manual* and training conferences; Mark DeJesus, *Inside Out Transformation,* as well as 1-½ years of attending his weekly teachings; Sharon Lewis, *Healing School Level 1 – A Course in Inner Healing,* plus *Healing School Level 2– A Course in Inner Healing,* as well as Level 1 and 2 healing schools; and Francis and Judith McNutt, *School of Healing Prayer, Level II.*

Reformation Center – "Restoring God's Original Design"

Bradenton, Florida

If you are interested in scheduling Linda to speak, host a *Transformation Healing* conference, or to let us know how reading *Designed for Destiny* has transformed your life, please email us at:

info@ReformationCenter.net

Website: www.ReformationCenter.net

www.LindaSantangelo.com

Please follow us on Facebook and YouTube:

www.facebook.com/linsantangelo (public page)

https://www.youtube.com/user/linsantangelo

Please visit our website to listen to some 1–2 minute testimonies of inner healing at:

www.ReformationCenter.net/testimonies

Additional 1–2 minute testimonies may be found on YouTube:

https://www.youtube.com/user/linsantangelo

Testimony means 'do again'. As you hear what God has done for others, it builds faith to believe He can 'do it again' for you!

Inner healing sessions are provided by our team at Reformation Center. Members of the Transformation Healing team are not professional licensed counselors. They are Spirit–filled Christians administering the love of God to help people achieve freedom and wholeness.

Prayer

Lord, my prayer is for those who have come to understand they have a destiny. When they discover what they have been designed to fulfill, I declare their destiny will lead them to great fulfillment and joy.

I also declare nothing in heaven or earth will hinder this next move of God coming on the earth, and *everyone* will take their rightful places, walking in the fullness of their destiny.

It's time to become the bride without spot or blemish so we can become the mature sons of God the earth is groaning for! It's time to become as Jesus is on the earth and do the greater works He told us we would do. I release power and authority to the Body of Christ to rise up and take their rightful place, walking in love, unity, and honoring one another.

In Jesus' mighty name, Amen!

ALL THE DAYS ORDAINED FOR ME
WERE WRITTEN IN YOUR BOOK BEFORE
ONE OF THEM CAME TO BE.
PSALM 139:16 (NIV)

Made in the USA
Columbia, SC
21 August 2018